YAYA'S STORY

PAUL STOLLER

YAYA'S STORY

The Quest for Well-Being in the World

THE UNIVERSITY OF CHICAGO PRESS
Chicago and London

PAUL STOLLER is professor of anthropology at West Chester University. He is the author of many books, most recently *Stranger in the Village of the Sick* and *The Power of the Between*, the latter published by the University of Chicago Press.

The University of Chicago Press, Chicago 60637
The University of Chicago Press, Ltd., London
© 2014 by The University of Chicago
All rights reserved. Published 2014.
Printed in the United States of America

23 22 21 20 19 18 17 16 15 14   1 2 3 4 5

DOI: 10.7208/Chicago/9780226178967.001.0001

Library of Congress Cataloging-in-Publication Data

Stoller, Paul, author.
    Yaya's story : the quest for well-being in the world / Paul Stoller.
        pages   cm
    Includes bibliographical references and index.
    ISBN 978-0-226-17879-0 (hardcover : alkaline paper) —
    ISBN 978-0-226-17882-0 (paperback : alkaline paper) —
    ISBN 978-0-226-17896-7 (e-book)   1. Stoller, Paul.   2. Songhai (African people)—Niger—Biography.   3. Nigeriens—New York (State)—New York—Biography.   4. Anthropologists—United States—Biography.   5. Interracial friendship—Case studies.   I. Title.
    F128.9.A24S761 2014
    301.092—dc23
    [B]

                                                    2014000536

♾ This paper meets the requirements of ANSI/NISO Z39.48-1992
(Permanence of Paper).

Frontispiece: Adamu Jenitongo, sohanci of Tillabéri, Niger. Photo by the author.

Stories are for those late hours in the night when you can't remember how you got from where you were to where you are. Stories are for an eternity, when memory is erased, when there is nothing to remember except the story.

— Tim O'Brien, *The Things They Carried*, 1990

CONTENTS

ACKNOWLEDGMENTS

The idea that writing is a solitary pursuit is partially true. Writers must find time and space to create their various works. But as all writers know, the solitary pursuit of text is one of many steps they must take to create and produce a published work. In the case of academic works, research and analysis precede the creation of draft text. Once that draft is ready, scholars usually send it to colleagues for comments. Comments in hand, scholars then revise the manuscript and prepare it for submission to a publisher. The publisher then finds experts to evaluate the text, provide additional comments, and make recommendations. If the recommendations are positive, publisher committees meet to discuss the project and make a final recommendation. If that recommendation is positive, the publisher offers a contract, and the manuscript goes into editing, during which editorial changes are suggested and implemented, which means that page proofs can then be generated, read, and corrected, all of which leads to publication. During this process the publisher hones its marketing strategy, crafting promotional copy in order to advertise the forthcoming publication. After a year the book is finally published.

Many people, then, are involved in the miraculous process through which an idea is transformed into a book, which means, of course, that any scholar, this one included, is indebted to institutions for research funding and to trusted colleagues, friends, and family for ever-necessary guidance. Such funding and guidance is needed if the final product is going to sing its song for a long period of time.

Yaya's Story is the result of many years of ethnographic research in the Republic of Niger and New York City. For granting me funds to engage in field research, I am grateful to the US Department of Education (Fulbright Research Program), the American Philosophical Foundation, the NATO Postdoctoral Fellowship in Science Program, the Wenner-Gren Foundation for Anthropological Research, the National Science Foundation, and West Chester University (the Faculty Development and College of Arts and Science research programs). For funds that provided time for writing, I acknowledge the John Simon Guggenheim Foundation; the School for Advanced Research in Santa Fe, New Mexico; the National Endowment for the Humanities; and West Chester University.

Yaya's Story emerged from a paper I delivered at a conference, the "Moral Borders of Self and Other: Migration, Reconciliation, and Human Wellbeing," that was convened by A. David Napier and Angela Hobart in June 2011 at Monte Verita in Ascona, Switzerland. Angela Hobart's Centro Incontri Umani sponsored the conference. I thank A. David Napier and Angela Hobart for their gracious invitation, commentary, and support. Feedback from a supportive and interdisciplinary audience sparked my imagination and convinced me to think more deeply about the issue of well-being in social life. Ongoing dialogue convinced me that I should transform the paper into a book-length manuscript. And so I did. For their comments and conversations on a very long path of discovery, I thank Michael Adelberg, Ruth Behar, Paul Clough, Valerian DeSousa, Jean-Paul Dumont, Jim Fernandez, Alma Gottlieb, Philip Graham, Sten Hagberg, Ulf Hannerz, Mark Harris, Brita Hermelin, Shahram Khosravi, Jerome Lewis, Christos Lynteris, Nick Mai, Marie Mauzé, Pauline Napier, Kirin Narayan, David Nugent, Nigel Rapport, Rodney Reynolds, Victoria Sultana, Barbara Tedlock, Dennis Tedlock, Gina Ulysse, Anna-Maria Volkmann, and Helena Wulff. For their ongoing support and inspiration I thank members of my family, Mitchell and Sheri Stoller, Lauren Stoller, Betsy Stoller, Beverly Gendelman, Melina McConatha, and Lauren McConatha. Since this book is about the future, I especially acknowledge Helena Mc-Conatha Rosle, eight years old, whose wondrous apprehension of the world is an inspiration, and Roxanne McConatha Spellman, eight months old, who represents the dawn of a new era. Sarah Alderman, Anna Mariella Bacigalupo, and Valerian De-Sousa read the entire manuscript, and their comments proved to be helpful. Comments from the University of Chicago Press's two anonymous readers were perceptive and quite useful. They have improved the quality of this text. Every writer appreciates good copyediting. The coherence and readability of this text are due in large measure to the masterly touch of Dawn Hall.

I would also like to thank three other people who have been central to my development as a scholar and a person. More than twenty-five years ago, T. David Brent risked publishing an unconventional book by a little-known author. So began a professional and personal friendship that has stood the test of time. I am forever grateful for David's trust in me, and hope this latest book reaffirms that trust. John Chernoff's friendship, advice, and love of life have always clarified for me the essential elements of living in the world. Our regular discussions have always steered me in fruitful directions. Finally, Jasmin Tahmaseb McConatha has made me a better person, scholar, and writer. Our ongoing conversations about what's important have given texture and direction to this book and to the meaning of my life.

PROLOGUE

THE STORY OF *Yaya's Story*

We are all restless at various points in our lives. Feelings of restlessness often develop from an existential itch that changing life circumstances provoke. Who among us has not had the urge to do something different, to follow a new path, or to feel the life-altering spark of something new?

During my time in the Republic of Niger, my teacher of things Songhay, the late Adamu Jenitongo, liked to tell me that the most elusive element of human being is the capacity to be, as he put it, "comfortable in your skin." Such comfort is usually fleeting. It is an unstable state that shifts with moments in time and ever-changing social and cultural contexts. In large measure the elusiveness of this comfort also defines the quest for well-being in the world. It is perhaps the desire for well-being that makes us restless.

Yaya's Story is about a life of restlessness, of trying something new, of taking risks. His story is about the quest to be comfortable in his skin. The tale of his quest presents lessons for us all. What meaning can we derive from our ever-shifting attempt to experience the comfort of well-being in the world?

The life stories in this work evoke other life stories—those of Yaya's anthropologist as well as those of anyone who happens to read this book. Stories can sometimes connect writers to readers in profound ways, reminding us of the times when we have been in lonely places—everywhere and nowhere places—where the story provides us a measure of genuinely appreciated and deeply treasured comfort.

: : :

I first met Yaya Harouna in February 1998. Like many of the art traders I encountered during my years of ethnographic fieldwork in New York City, Yaya had made the pilgrimage to Mecca, an accomplishment that earned him the prestigious title El Hajj—a denotation of the economic success, physical strength, and spiritual devotion of those who make the arduous journey to the Kaaba, Islam's most sacred site.

We met on a cold winter afternoon at the Warehouse, a six-story storage facility situated near the Hudson River in New York's Chelsea neighborhood. On that day the Warehouse stood tall and imposing amid a gritty New York City urbanscape: dingy delicatessens in front of which loitered homeless men wrapped in winter rags and drinking coffee; dim dry cleaning shops over-stuffed with bundles of dirty clothes piled like heaps of garbage on the counter; downscale Indian restaurants, smelling of curry, the grime of which filmed their front windows. One block from the Warehouse there is a large garage where mechanics repair Yellow cabs, as well as a scrap metal yard strewn with the twisted and rusty remains of a thousand vehicles.

The Warehouse, which is also known as Chelsea Mini Storage, is on Twenty-Seventh Street between Eleventh and Twelfth Avenues. It is a massive building that consumes one Manhattan block. On the day I first met Yaya, small trucks and Econoline vans were backed up to the docking bays that lined the south side of the Warehouse. Men in heavy coats and ski caps loaded and unloaded cargo—African masks and statues, bolts of printed cloth, and large sacks filled with grain. Clusters of other men, Africans all, swaddled for protection from the winter wind, huddled just inside the glass door entrance to the Warehouse.

On that February day, I opened the door and greeted the men in French.

"Welcome," they chanted as they extended their hands.

"You're El Hajj Abdou's friend, no?" I had met El Hajj Abdou

FIGURE 1.
The Warehouse in New York City. Photo by the author.

Harouna, who was Yaya's older brother, a year earlier. He immediately took me to the Warehouse.

"I am," I said. "I'm here to visit El Hajj Abdou."

"This is good," a thick man with a square face stated. "Abdou will be pleased."

One step into the Warehouse marked a distinct existential transformation. Moments before I had taken in some of Manhattan's grittiest streets—the real urban deal. Now I walked into a dim, dank space with a corridor populated by African art traders and stuffed with their goods—wooden statues and masks that smelled of smoke. They, too, greeted "El Hajj's" friend. After a short walk through the corridor, I entered a square open space filled with shabby garage sale sofas and tables and bordered by market stalls that displayed African art. Some traders specialized in beaded Cameroonian pieces; others featured the lifelike masks that the Guro people of Côte d'Ivoire carved. Abdou's stall was at the west end of this square room, the back of the space, where another corridor led to the bathroom. He sold masks and statuary from coastal West Africa, but he also displayed the art of the Tuareg, the nomads of the Sahara—red and black leather camel saddles with the tall pummels shaped like the Southern Cross; daggers and swords sheathed in red and black leather cases; and long leather pillows, some red, some yellow, that had been trimmed at each end with red leather tassels.

Abdou Harouna, a tall lean man then perhaps in his late sixties, sat in one of four chairs that had been positioned opposite his stall. He wore a dull gray shirt over dark gray trousers. The dome of his shaved head gleamed in the dull light. The tight stretch of black skin over his high cheekbones gave him a rather severe expression that was balanced by an ever-present playful twinkle in his eyes.

"Monsieur Paul," he said extending his hand to me. "Are you still among the living?"

"I give thanks for life, El Hajj," I responded, taking his calloused hand in mine.

"Iri koy; gabi koy."

"Yes," he responded. "God is the owner of strength. But you were away for too long. We didn't hear from you." He smiled. "Thank you for your visit. You are not lost to us."

Abdou sat between two elderly gentlemen, both of whom had donned elaborate robes, the grand boubou. He introduced me to Moussa Ibrahim, the man to his left, who wore a white damask boubou with elaborate gold embroidery stitched around the neck. Looking like a multistranded figure eight, a complex wisdom knot, also stitched in gold thread, covered a deep center pocket. The red fez atop his large head gave way to a round and smooth face. Moussa, who had also made the pilgrimage to Mecca, was, to say the least, stout, but the ample boubou transformed his fleshy body into an imposing figure. Seated to Abdou's left was a slender man with a thin bony face and a furrowed brow—El Hajj Mounkaila Sidi. He wore an unembroidered powder blue boubou—and a frown. The rise under his lip suggested a lump of chewing tobacco.

We exchanged greetings in French, for both of Abdou's colleagues hailed from Mali and did not speak the Songhay language.

"But we have heard you speak Abdou's language. You have shown us respect and that's good," Moussa asserted.

El Hajj Abdou pointed to the only empty chair in the line and asked me to sit down. As several men walked by en route to the bathroom, Abdou began to talk about selling African art. He bemoaned the recent trend in which ignorant traders had flooded the market with mass-produced and crudely carved reproductions of popular masks and statues. "There are so many *akwabas*," he lamented, referring to the round-faced fertility dolls the Asante of Ghana carved, "that the real ones have lost their value."

Mounkaila's frown deepened. "I know. There are so many bad pieces that our clients no longer have confidence in us." He shook his head. "Thirty years ago, it was better—easier to make a living."

"That's true," said Moussa. "In the past, I made good profits and I invested them in inventory—more masks and statues. Back then the market here in New York was very, very good. Now it's hard to find good pieces in Africa. So now I invest in gems—silver, gold, diamonds—and in transport. In Mali I've got trucks—very good money in that."

"I've done some of that," Abdou added, "but my passion is the art. Even if it is more difficult now, I love the masks and statues. I like being around them, and I like the people who bring these pieces from Africa to America."

The discussion drifted to techniques some traders used to make average reproductions more like "original" works of art. They mentioned time-honored practices like burying a wooden statue or mask in a termite hill or covering a work with millet gruel and letting roosters peck at it. They also debated the whys and wherefores of Minwax, beeswax filler, and the services of professional restorers, whose fees had skyrocketed in recent years. Moussa extolled the virtues of his son, who had success-fully taken over much of his international business dealings. Mounkaila complained about his son who, like the son of El Hajj Moussa, had assumed much of the responsibility of his father's affairs. "That boy," the acerbic Mounkaila said while shaking his head, "is lazy."

The call for the sunset prayer disrupted an animated discus-sion. Without saying anything, Mounkaila stood up and made his way to the bathroom to perform the necessary ablutions that prepare one for prayer. Soon a stream of traders, including Moussa, followed suit.

Abdou playfully slapped my shoulder. "I'll wait awhile—too crowded in there." He paused a moment. "Paul," he wondered, "when are you going to become a Muslim?"

"There are many paths to God's house, El Hajj," I responded. "What's important," I said, remembering what Adamu Jenitongo once told me, "is what you have in your heart."

Abdou slapped me on the shoulder. "That, Paul, is the clear truth."

Just then two men wearing dress trousers and overcoats carried in two large cartons filled with fresh fruit—bananas, oranges, and red delicious apples. "Okay, everyone, take one piece of fruit."

When they came to me, I hesitated.

"Don't you want some fruit?" one of them asked.

"Of course I do," I answered. I picked out a banana and was about to peel it when I realized what was going on. My visit had occurred during the month of Ramadan, during which Muslims fast from sunup to sundown. This fast means that no food or liquid—even saliva—should make its way down your throat. After a long and difficult day of fasting, young traders distributed fruit to everyone so they might break the fast softly and effec-tively.

Soon the community of believers had converged on the

mosque—a windowless rectangular room covered with cheap rugs—leaving me alone on my chair. How lovely, I thought, that someone in this community took it upon himself to make sure that every believer would have fruit with which to break the fast. Who had paid for the fruit? Who had arranged to have it delivered?

In short order the traders returned from the mosque. We gathered as a group in the square room, each holding her or his piece of fruit. Amid broken-down furniture and under the gaze of thousands of non-Muslim masks and statues, we all gave thanks for our lives. We peeled our fruit, shook hands, exchanged greetings, smiled and laughed, celebrating the triumph of making it through yet another day in good health.

El Hajj Abdou took my hand and smiled. "Paul, "he said, taking in the scene, "this is our African community." He then introduced to me a tall, thick, and squared-faced man with penetrating eyes—his brother, Yaya.

Yaya shook my hand, smiled, and asked me to sit down.

"My brother has told me that you speak our language," he said in Songhay. "He told me about your work." He nodded his head. "I think we'll be friends," he said. "If you talk to me about your work, I'll talk to you about mine."[1]

: : :

Yaya's Story is really the tale of two men, who, separated by ethnicity, language, culture, profession, and personal circumstance, bridged their considerable differences to reach a remarkable point of existential convergence, a deep dialogue that brought on a moving moment of profound mutual understanding. The stories in the book recount adventures experienced along two distinct life paths. Yaya's path followed the twists and turns of contemporary commerce. My path followed the sinuous trails of anthropology. Our life histories trigger other stories about global commerce, cultural alienation, transnational migration, ethnographic fieldwork, spirit possession, and sorcery. In time our winding paths finally crossed in New York City, where we met and built a friendship that gradually transcended the profound differences that separated us. Taken together, the narratives in this book highlight the wonders of human resilience and celebrate our potential for mutual understanding.

The reader may wonder why a book titled *Yaya's Story* also includes the tale of "his anthropologist." There are two reasons for this textual choice. The first reason stems from the practical truths of storytelling. The storyteller's tale always implicates the storyteller's biography. As Adamu Jenitongo once told me: "If you want to tell my story, you'll have to tell your story as well."

The second reason is more philosophical. What is anthropology all about? For many practitioners anthropology is partially about the refinement of method and theory, which deepens our comprehension of the human condition. More often than not this orientation produces texts that fine-tune current theories and methods. These works are important, but how long will they remain open to the world? Will they be read and discussed five, ten, or twenty years from now? Anthropology, however, is also about the attempt to recount tales that underscore the key elements—hate and love, fear and courage, betrayal and loyalty, to name a few—that define our humanity. Anthropologists can sometimes write narratives that connect readers to writers, triggering mutual understandings that make the world a little bit sweeter. These texts have the capacity to remain open to the world, stories that future generations will read and discuss.

Yaya's Story is an attempt to produce a text that will remain open to the world. Part 1, "A Life Story in Commerce," portrays Yaya's first home, Belayara, a famous market town in western Niger. In this part of the book, the narratives recount how Yaya and his two brothers, Abdou and Daouda, slipped into the trading life. Their specialization in African art—wooden masks, antique weapons, silver jewelry, and wooden and terra-cotta figurines—eventually took all three of them to the Warehouse in New York City. Part 2, "A Life Story in Anthropology," describes the forces that came together to compel me, a child of suburban Washington, DC, to follow the anthropological path. It describes how a life in anthropology is shaped through reading, professional interchange, fieldwork, and personal circumstance, a path that eventually led me to New York City and the West African art traders of the Warehouse. Part 3, "Awakenings," describes how the experience of serious illness profoundly changes a person's life, eventually bringing Yaya and me, men defined through difference, to a moment of profound existential convergence. At that moment, we both understood for the first time how the quest for well-being had profoundly shaped the existential texture of our lives.

ONE

A LIFE STORY IN COMMERCE

1 ::: BELAYARA

Niger is a hard land. When you first confront Niger's heat, it grabs you like an angry wrestler. The air feels like a fire burning close to your skin. Even in the cool season, the sun is intense. The unremitting presence of such searing heat creates a rugged, parched vista: vast clay plains that pancake to distant rocky buttes that give way to other stretches of tawny plains that abut to yet another line of rocky buttes. Clusters of scrub, an occasional acacia or baobab break the flat sameness of the brown haze of rock and clay. A few clusters of green in the distance sometimes mark the presence of a water hole and perhaps a well-situated village whose inhabitants can exploit the regular presence of water in an arid land. When you travel toward Niger's northern provinces, the vegetation thins out. There the plains are often strewn with rock. Buttes give way to dunes. Eventually, you cross an invisible border and find yourself in the Sahara. No matter where you are, the Harmattan, the desert wind, swooshes across the plains, kicking up dust devils here and there, carrying with it the stale odor of dust.

: : :

When you travel to Belayara, which is only sixty-six kilometers northeast of Niamey, Niger's capital city, you see vast stretches of those desiccated rock-strewn plains, the flat monotony of which is occasionally broken by buttes that rise up along the horizon. In Niamey, your taxi, a Toyota minivan, makes its way to the Wadata market, which is near the intersection of the Boulevard Mali Bero and the N25, a "paved" road that snakes its way from Niamey's northeast quadrant toward Fillingue. The market consists of a series of dirt paths that divide row upon row of mud brick and crudely crafted wooden stalls. Roofs crafted from corrugated tin or daub and wattle protect the stalls from the elements. The market is densely packed with buyers and sellers who trade all sorts of goods transported on donkey-pulled carts, burdened donkeys, or loaded camels. As you pass the market on the N25 its din gradually fades as you head toward Niamey's outskirts. A police checkpoint marks the edge of the city beyond which you get your first glimpse of the bush's vast emptiness.

At first glance the landscape is marred with garbage—mounds of it line the road. Beyond the heaps of trash lie innumerable shards of discarded plastic bags that the wind has wrapped around scrub brush, scraggly acacia trees, and an occasional tamarind. Niamey's uncultivated "suburbs," which seem devoid of village life, have become the capital city's dumping grounds. Given Niamey's ever-increasing population, it takes some time to clear the trash fields. As the taxi enters the bush, the road deteriorates. Frequently you must leave the pavement for the older dirt road to avoid axle-breaking potholes. The older road takes you to a village of conical mud and thatch huts, a ramshackle market of stalls fashioned from sticks and woven grass, and a well-manicured mosque marked by the deep green of a freshly painted minaret. Dressed in rags, a cluster of children will smile and wave as you pass them. They are soon obscured in a cloud of dust—the wake of the vehicle. Leaving the village, the taxi soon returns to a trackless bush of empty fields, rocky stretches of scrub plain, and the outcroppings of sandstone buttes. After crossing ten kilometers or so of rocky plain, you come to another village, which looks surprisingly like the previous settlement—mud-brick houses and huts, a dusty market space of empty lean-to stalls, and a well-kept mosque. As the taxi heads farther north and east, the plains get sandier and dunes rise in the distance like so many loaves of bread. The road conditions continue to de-

teriorate. Crumbling edges and gaping craters make it ever more necessary to follow the winding ways of the old dirt road. Where a washed-out bridge appears, the taxi has to cross a deep-sanded wadi—a good place to get stuck. If the driver has packed metal planks to put under the buried tires, it's relatively easy to get free. Perhaps ten kilometers from Belayara you begin to see people streaming toward market. Some ride donkeys or camels. Some market goers ride carts loaded with firewood. Dressed in colorful printed cloth, women walk with pots balanced on their heads.

When the taxi finally gets to Belayara on market day, you see a village clogged with huge transport trucks, minivan taxis, cars, people, camels, donkeys, horses, and cows—so many cows. On the outskirts of town you pass an empty primary school. Farther on, there is the mosque. In the town center a cement building whose whitewashed walls have been dulled by exposure to wind and dust houses the post office. Nearby is a bar and restaurant. Just beyond the bar toward the north stretches a large and vibrant market, a series of sandy paths bordered by hundreds of market stalls where merchants offer colorful Songhay blankets;

mats woven from dried grass; long leather pillows, dyed red and yellow with leather tassels; onions, garlic, tomatoes, and greens (in season); spices; clay pots, porcelain plates, knives, and forks; Dutch wax print cloth; kola nuts; and tobacco. You can even find furniture—desks, chairs, bed frames, and mattresses.

Beyond the market stall area, there is a wide-open space where livestock—cows, sheep, and goats—is bought and sold. Herders travel for days to bring livestock to Belayara. Buyers from Nigeria and Benin travel for days to purchase some of the best cattle in West Africa. They eventually load the cattle into large trucks that will deliver their cargo to southern markets where they will gather a good price and a handsome profit.

By late afternoon, the market begins to wind down. Fully loaded trucks leave the vehicle depot, which is situated next to the livestock space. Headed for distant destinations, the trucks rumble onto the paved road. Stuffed with people and goods, overloaded minivans putter along the road. Perhaps they will make it home without a breakdown? Fully loaded donkey-drawn carts, camels, and donkeys begin their slow return to home villages. Men, women, and children follow these beasts of burden. They, too, carry bundles of goods. Just before your own return, you go to the bar, order a cold drink, and repair to a shady courtyard, where you find musicians who play lutes and sing Songhay epics—all for a modest fee.

As you climb into the taxi for your return, the market din subsides and you notice that Belayara has begun its slow return to a normal state—a sleepy town on the road to Fillingue, the seat of the provincial government.

: : :

Like most markets in West Africa the one in Belayara has been shaped through gender and ethnicity. Gender usually determines what you sell. Women sell fresh and dried spices, milk and cheese, and handicrafts like woven baskets, fans, and mats.

FIGURE 3. A Belayara musician reciting the Epic of Mali Bero, 2009.
Photo by the author.

Sometimes women sell peanut oil, but so do men. Men sell blankets and bulk printed cloth as well as rock salt brought in from mines deep in the Sahara. They also sell leather goods—wallets, sandals, hassocks, and pillows—and fuels like kerosene. Men also own the rights to buy and sell livestock.

Ethnicity also plays a role in market dynamics. In Belayara region there are four major ethnic groups. The principal group is Songhay-Zarma, direct and indirect descendants of the Songhay Empire, a medieval state that ruled much of West Africa. The Songhay-Zarma population is complemented by two semi-nomadic groups, the Fulan, cattle herders known for their love of the freedom you find in isolated stretches of bush, and the Tuareg, desert nomads known for their past marauding and bellicosity. Finally, Hausa-speaking populations, long known for their long-distance trading, migrated to the region to exploit regional markets.

At the market Songhay people sell foodstuffs and spices, blankets, and are livestock brokers. Fulan people sell cows, milk, and butter. Hausa people butcher meat and cook market kabobs. They also sell leather goods. Tuaregs buy and sell camels, sheep and goats, firewood, and rock salt. If Tuareg smiths are present they will sell hoes, knives, spears, boxes covered with tooled leather, and silver jewelry. Yoruba from Nigeria sell hardware—forks, spoons, pots, cooking knives, nails, and screws.[1]

As a characteristic market town the population of Belayara is not only multiethnic but multilingual as well. Accordingly, many of the market-savvy residents in Belayara speak not only Songhay but also Hausa, the major trade language in West Africa, and Tamasheq, the language of the Tuareg nomads. Put another way, the size and reputation of the market makes the small town of Belayara a cosmopolitan space. Many of its inhabitants have traveled far and wide following long-established trading routes as well as those more recent.

If you grew up in Belayara, the market and its ethos would have had a deep impact on your worldview. From an early age Yaya and his brothers, Abdou, and Daouda, learned that the trading life was an honorable one, a life that could bring a person both money and social prestige. They learned that truly prosperous merchants not only enjoyed material prosperity but also possessed "wealth in people," a person with a wide network of people whom you could trust.[2]

From talking with senior traders, the young Yaya learned that Islam is central to trading practices. The key to successful trading, according to the hadith of the Prophet Muhammad, devolved from relations based upon mutual trust. If a trader extended credit to trading partner, he or she would expect that the

FIGURE 4. A blanket trader in the Belayara market. Photo by the author.

credit to be repaid. If a trader purchased goods from a partner, he or she would expect that partner to ship those goods.[3]

And so growing up in Belayara exposed Yaya and his brothers to the West African culture of trade, the lure of the good sale, the adventure of travel, and also to the considerable comforts of home. When traders returned to the market from long trips to Niamey, Niger's capital; to Lagos, Nigeria; or Lomé, Togo; and most especially the thriving metropolis of Abidjan, Côte d'Ivoire, they would recount their adventures in distant worlds of wonder—the food of youthful imagination gave young men the appetite for travel. But they also stressed how good it was to return to the familiar smells and sights of home. What could be better than to return to the warm embrace of their mothers and fathers, aunts and uncles, and brothers and sisters?

Abdou, Yaya's older brother, left Belayara in the late 1950s. A fraternal relative invited him to work in Abidjan, which, at that time, was a fabled commercial city. The young Abdou sold watches and bracelets in Abidjan markets and following the instructions of his elders saved as much money as he could. In time, he had the capital to buy and sell his own goods—soap, hard candy, chewing gum, homespun cloth, bracelets, and cheap watches. Because of his entrepreneurial talents, he gradually expanded his network of suppliers and clients. By the time he was in his early twenties Abdou had fashioned himself a place in Abidjan's economic life. He had become a trader of *nyama-nyama*, a little bit of everything.

Although Abdou had learned to speak, read, and write French in elementary school, he saw his future along the path of commerce. Yaya, too, attended primary school and did well enough to become a student at the middle school in Fillingue, the provincial capital. There, he boarded with a family that housed and fed him—not always so well. Despite being far from kith and kin, Yaya liked studying French, math, and science, and also took to the study of English, which was required in middle school. Like his father and older brother, he made sure to recite his prayers five times a day, and when the month of Ramadan occurred during the school year, he fasted from sunup to sundown.

By the end of middle school, in 1970, Yaya, now a teenager, decided to forgo his formal studies. At the invitation of his brother, who by now had married and had become a successful Abidjan trader and the head of a growing household, Yaya traveled to Abidjan. It was his first step on the path of trade. Despite these adventures, he admitted to me during our conversations at the Warehouse or at the Malcolm Shabazz Harlem Market, he always looked forward to return visits to Belayara.

For his part, Daouda excelled in school. Yaya's younger brother was among the best students at the Belayara primary school. He won entry into the Fillingue middle school, where he impressed the teachers. In his last year of middle school, Daouda received high marks on his brevet, the exam you must pass to enter a lycée or a normal school. Because he wanted to be a primary school teacher, Daouda decided to attend an École Normale. By the time Yaya had begun to buy and sell Tuareg jewelry in Abidjan—silver Agadez crosses and beautiful silver rings—Daouda had graduated from normal school. He found some temporary positions in isolated villages but couldn't find a more permanent position in a larger town. Eventually, he, too, decided on a life in commerce. He left Niger and joined his brothers in Abidjan. Like his brothers, he looked forward to return visits to Belayara.

2 ::: THREE BROTHERS AND THE WORK OF ART

With the arrival of Daouda in Abidjan, the three brothers began to prosper. Abdou took an interest in wooden masks crafted by ethnic groups in the Côte d'Ivoire. From Abidjan he traveled upcountry into the forest to buy Guro and Baule masks. When he had amassed a substantial collection of masks and figurines, he flew to Paris, where he sold them to other African traders or to tourists at the flea market at the Port de Clignancourt.

The quick sale of the collection produced handsome profits. Abdou used these to invest more extensively in the highly stylized masks and figurines of the Guro and Baule peoples. In time, he brought his inventory to New York City, where the profits proved to be more substantial than those in Paris. As his inventory grew in size, he shipped containers of masks and figurines to Port Elizabeth, New Jersey, where they cleared customs. He then brought the goods to the Warehouse where he consigned them to trusted couriers who would take them to private clients or to African American trade shows. These sales also produced substantial profits that Abdou used to buy more masks and figurines, build houses in Abidjan and Belayara, purchase transport vehicles, and buy precious gems—mostly rubies and diamonds.

By the late 1980s Abdou had hit his stride. He had a home and farms in Belayara, a house in Niamey, Niger's capital city, and an extensive compound in Abidjan. He had been to Mecca two times, had three wives, and more children than he could count. Every year, he spent several months in North America, mostly

FIGURE 5.
A typical
Guro mask.
Photo by the
author.

in New York City, but sometimes he visited clients in Chicago, New Orleans, Atlanta, and Montreal. He had become a highly respected and prosperous man who had amassed "wealth in money" and "wealth in people."[1] Despite his extensive travel, Abdou always found time to return to Belayara.

Daouda, the former primary school teacher, took a commercial interest in antique tools and weapons, horse and camel saddles, and household items like stools, neck rests, and chairs. He started small in Abidjan but eventually amassed a substantial inventory of items, which enabled him to shepherd his pieces first to France and then in 1995 to New York City. Unlike Abdou, he preferred to do all of his business in New York City. Traveling to outposts like Chicago, Indianapolis, or Dallas did not interest him very much. In time his family also grew—two wives, many children, and houses in Belayara, Niamey, and Abidjan. Although he could afford to travel to Mecca, he practiced a more relaxed Islam, which meant that he hadn't yet made the expensive pilgrimage.

Yaya wanted to sell objects that Tuareg smiths crafted. These included finely etched silver rings, some new and some quite old; and silver and brass bracelets, also finely etched with geometric designs. He also collected the famous Croix d'Agadez, a tooled cross, inspired by the Southern Cross, that had as many as thirty design variations. When Yaya had put together a substantial inventory of these objects, he, too, decided to try his hand in the North American market, which by all reports, including those of his older brother Abdou, seemed ripe for exploration.

: : :

The context and global forces that enabled Abdou, Daouda, and Yaya to exploit the African art markets in North America had been set in motion generations before the births of the three brothers from Belayara. The conditions that gave African art both aesthetic and economic value have deep roots in the west-

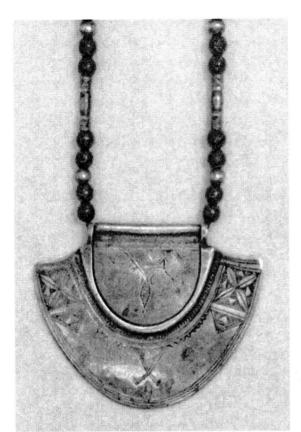

FIGURE 6.
The Croix
d'Agadez.
Photo by
the author.

ern aesthetic tradition. Why would someone want to buy a work of Africa art? "Because," Yaya once said to me, "it's old and pleasing to the eye and people will pay for that."

Considering their long history as traders who understand economic conditions and trends, Yaya and his colleagues understood that "art" did not come into existence without a market. The great art auction houses, Sotheby's and Christie's, were both founded in the eighteenth century. Indeed, markets for high arts expanded considerably in the nineteenth century—especially toward the end of that epoch. Impressionism, which was an artistic revolt against the aesthetic hegemony of French academic art, was central to the economic development of modern art. The impressionists refused to show their art through "academic" channels, preferring to exhibit their work at private gatherings. These gatherings, which culminated in their last group show in 1886, catapulted the impressionists into the avant-garde. The success of this bold move also resulted in incomes that enabled many impressionists to work on their art full time.[2]

> The impressionists show that financial success for artists was possible through the activities of key dealers and friendly critics, independent of state of official patronage. [Raymonde] Moulin points out that Pissarro, Degas, Monet, and Renoir and the other Impressionists earned incomes commensurate with those earned by civil servants. . . . Their "outrageous" art, when sold to discriminating, adventurous collectors, produced middle-class incomes for the artists.[3]

Stuart Plattner describes how impressionism established a new network among avant-garde artists, dealers, critics, and collector-connoisseurs. This network set the cultural and economic foundation for twentieth-century avant-garde movements (futurism, cubism, abstract expressionism, minimalism, conceptual art, and so on). The recognition of economic incentive and the production of value did not diminish the significance of an object's transcendental power—a source of its economic importance. Because they understood how the mystique of transcendent art would enhance value, dealers arranged their wares in displays that mimicked the great museums—high ceilings, white walls, dim lighting, and minimal presentation—all to isolate the object's aesthetic qualities. Indeed, this aesthetic is sill with us. A visit to most galleries in Manhattan would reinforce this aesthetic concept. Plattner describes a photo of an art gallery in Saint Louis. "The huge spaces, high ceilings, and dramatic exhibition style are designed to impress the viewer with the museum quality of the work."[4] "Museum quality," of course, also means high prices.

The aesthetic and economic story of high art is echoed in the development of taste for so-called primitive art, which refers loosely to the pieces that Yaya and his brothers brought to American markets. Shelly Errington traces the history of "primitive art" back to the famous Armory Show of 1913, which suddenly and spectacularly introduced modern art to America. The impact of that event eventually inspired rich patrons, especially Abby Aldrich Rockefeller, to create the Museum of Modern Art (MOMA) in 1929. Over time MOMA exhibitions legitimized avant-garde modern art, which, in turn, increased its cultural and economic value.[5]

In this cultural climate, Nelson Rockefeller began to collect "tribal art" from Oceania, Africa, and the Americas. After his appointment in 1950 as MOMA's director, the museum paid serious attention to primitive art, which, in turn, prompted a series of "tribal" exhibitions, which increased the public desire for and value of objects made by nameless artists in faraway lands. The legitimized exposure corresponded to new critical appreciation of the aesthetic qualities of tribal art. In short order, dealers bought new kinds of objects and showcased them in their museum-like galleries, a trend that compelled connoisseurs to visit these cutting-edge galleries and buy an "important" piece.

In 1957 the Museum of Primitive Art, comprised mostly of the Rockefeller collection, opened its doors. This development elevated the cultural and economic importance of tribal art in North America. The museum remained opened for twenty years.

> [The] two decades mark the golden age of primitive art's legitimacy. The existence of so many wonderful objects, beautifully exhibited and celebrated in fine arts museums as art, attested to the unproblematic nature of the category of

authentic primitive art. During the period liberal and right-thinking people admired and celebrated it. Art historians and anthropologists discovered primitive art as a worthy subject of study, and an increasing number of books and articles appeared on the topic. A few art history departments hired specialists in primitive art, and several Ph.D. programs in non-Western art were established and produced their first graduates; a number of major museums established departments and curatorial positions of primitive art. As an essential category, primitive was almost unchallenged.[6]

The Museum of Primitive Art closed to make way for the Michael Rockefeller wing of New York City's Metropolitan Museum of Art. By the time that wing opened in 1982, primitive art had found a prominent place in one of the world's leading institutions of art. The display of tribal objects in the Michael Rockefeller wing reproduced the aesthetic context long valorized in the world of aesthetics—high ceilings, open spaces, and minimal presentation. Freed from the conditions of their productions, the museum context gave these tribal objects a timeless quality.[7]

The legitimacy of tribal art may have received a boost from MOMA's 1984 exhibition "Primitivism" in 20th Century Art. The curators of the exhibition attempted to demonstrate how so-called primitive objects had inspired the greatest artists of the modern era. Georges Braque and Pablo Picasso, who collected tribal art, kept many of the pieces in their studios. Through the juxtaposition of primitive masks and statuettes to various works of modern art, the curators wanted viewers to see clear parallels in aesthetic form. In so doing, they wanted to suggest that primitive art was the inspiration for cubist and surrealist art. Such a theory, which a good number of scholars have found unconvincing, may have increased the cultural and economic value of non-Western objects of art. How wonderful it would be to own an object that had inspired Picasso![8]

In the wake of the *"Primitivism" in 20th Century Art* exhibition several new museums opened, including the revamped and re-housed Smithsonian National Museum of African Art and the Museum for African Art, which was first located on Sixty-Eighth Street in midtown Manhattan, then in SoHo, then in Long Island City. The museum will soon be housed permanently on the corner of Fifth Avenue and 110th Street.

This history of cultural and economic events helped to reinforce a set of aesthetic criteria for objects of primitive art. Curators and dealers created standards of authenticity. Since no one knew who had carved a particularly refined statuette or mask, curators linked provenance to an object's history of collection, sale, and exhibition. If well-known connoisseurs, artists, or dealers owned a piece, it would become an "important" piece of value. That value, of course, would increase even more if the object's plastic qualities conformed to the formal simplicity of modernist aesthetics.

: : :

Even though Yaya and his colleagues were not privy to the whys and wherefores of art history, they had learned enough from auction catalogs, museum exhibitions, and professional journals like *African Arts* to understand why a collector would be compelled to pay substantial sums for an old piece that a nameless African had used. Early on they learned that if a figurine had been doused with sacrificial blood, or if a mask had been danced, the value of the piece would be enhanced substantially. It was not unusual for me to witness African art traders in Niger, Côte d'Ivoire, Paris, and New York City studying and discussing the latest issues of *African Arts* or a recent Sotheby's sales catalog.

Although such study may have helped them to market their wares, it did not change their beliefs about the art objects or their fundamental approach to trading. Yaya told me that for him art was simply a commodity that had become generally desirable.

For Muslim men like Yaya African art is "wood" (wooden figurines and masks, called *bundu* in Songhay), "iron" (weapons and tools, called *guuru* in Songhay), and "mud" (pottery and terracotta sculpture, called *botigo* in Songhay).

Long before Yaya came into the world, Islam and the history of long-distance trading in West Africa had profoundly shaped the West African orientation to "wood," "iron," and "mud." In a previous work, *Money Has No Smell*, I described how Islam and the history of long-distance trading in West Africa had molded the economic and social practices of West African street vendors in Harlem.[9] Although West African art traders like Yaya are quite distinct from the street vendors described in that work, their ideas and expectations about display, trade, and marketing have been no less influenced by religion and history.

Like the Harlem vendors, art traders at the Warehouse tend to be members of West African ethnic groups—Sonninke, Hausa, and Wolof—that have long been the professional traders of West Africa.[10] From the eighteenth century to the present these groups have traded cloth, kola, tobacco, and beads throughout West Africa. Through trade they not only helped to expand the political reach of nascent West African states but also extended the reach of their religion—Islam.[11]

: : :

Yaya and his colleagues found themselves in a space between the history and economics of Western aesthetics and the practices of trade that formed the foundation of classical Islam. The tension between the two approaches to art, trade, and markets has been remarkably productive—a kind of a perfect storm. We have already explored how patterns of a Western aesthetic led to the development of taste and value for fine art. We now turn to the other side of the equation. How has Islam shaped the trading practices of men like Yaya?

From its very beginnings, Islam and merchant capital have

been inextricably linked. Commerce, in fact, has been central to the development and diffusions of Islam.[12] In the Prophet Muhammad's new world, the *Ummah* became a collection of human beings Allah protected. In theory, your allegiance to the Ummah pushed class divisions and ethnic identity to the background of social consciousness. In addition, Muhammad, whose wife, Khadija, was herself a prosperous merchant, recognized trade as an honorable profession. In his view expansion of trade would not only help the Ummah to prosper economically but also would enable it to increase its power and influence. What's more, trade, according to the Prophet Muhammad, should be straightforward and transparent. If trade were reliable, trustworthy, and honest, it would ensure harmonious social relations. In various passages of the Koran and the Sunnah, there are many statements about giving false oaths, correct weights, and goodwill in transactions. The Prophet Muhammad thought that contracts should be established clearly and comprehensively. He stood against monopolistic practices and forbade usury because these actions undermined commercial and social relations—which, for him, should not be considered as separate domains.[13] As pious Muslims, West African traders like Yaya have attempted to follow these traditional principles with, of course, a few refinements that fit in with contemporary economic and cultural circumstances.

The economic principles of Islam reinforce family solidarity, an important notion for Yaya and his brothers. These, in turn, generate the real and fictive kinship ties of West African trading families. Like all kinship systems, the rites and obligations in West African trading families are shaped by two major factors: age and gender. In 1971 Jean-Loup Amselle wrote about the trading families of the Kooroko of southern Mali. A Kooroko household head provides food, shelter, clothes, and tax money for the people in his compound, who, in turn, give him what they produce. In some circumstances the household head is also a *jula-*

ba, a successful trader who, from the comforts of his compound, manages a complex long-distance trading network. Kinspeople, affines, and friends keep the great trader well informed about changing market conditions—both close to and far away from home. If conditions were good, the great trader would send his *jula-ben* (literally trader-child—younger brothers, children, and his brothers' children) to distant markets to sell kola nut or buy cattle. In distant markets (Côte d'Ivoire, Ghana, France, or even New York City), hosts, who usually have blood or marriage ties to the great trader, receive the "children," making sure they are housed and plugged into local trading networks. Following a set of transactions, the "children" return home to report to their "father." They receive no payment for their trading efforts. In time the paternal kinsmen of the great trader may ask for economic independence, which is usually granted along with cash to start a new enterprise.

Sometimes great traders do not have a sufficient number of paternal kin to direct a long-distance enterprise. In these circumstances the jula-ba recruits his maternal kin, the children of his sisters, or friends who are not members of his personal kindred. No matter the extent of their blood-relatedness, the "children" must all observe the rights and obligations of the great trader's paternal kin. Accordingly, they receive no payment for their initial services. After several successful transactions, trader "children" may ask their "father" for a loan to buy new inventory. Although the "children" continue to perform services for the jula-ba, they have begun a contractual relationship with their "father."

During the first phase of the contractual relationship "children" must give their "father" two-thirds of their profits. If profits continue to flow in, the great traders may offer more credit. If the work of "children" does not produce a profit, the great traders will continue to support them, but will not give them another loan. Successful "children" give the great trader

50 percent of their profits. In time the "children" may themselves become prosperous, which means that eventually they take their leave from the great traders and become jula-ba themselves.[14]

: : :

These kinship contoured contractual relationships have persisted among West African traders like Yaya at the Warehouse. Core networks often consist of paternal and maternal kin linked to a great trader somewhere in West Africa. Other networks consist of unrelated traders who come from the same town or region. In New York City, though, shared ethnicity seems to play a more central role in the establishment and reinforcement of networks.[15] Whatever the composition of New York City trading networks, it is clear that participants, following the dictates of classical Islam, actively cooperate with one another.

On any given day New York City traders share market information, divide the costs of transport from Manhattan to points in the American countryside (called the "bush"), and extend credit to one another. The object, of course, is to move as much product ("wood," "iron," and "mud") as possible. Traders use the funds from the sale of art objects to reinvest in more "wood," but also in precious gems, real estate in the United States and in West Africa, and transport vehicles. Traders also send money to West Africa to support their extended families.

Like the West African street traders in Harlem, art traders like Yaya had to adjust their commercial practices to North American economic realities. They are sensitive to changing patterns of American consumption. In the early 1970s when Abdou, Yaya's older brother, first came to the United States to sell "wood," he was among a small number of West African art merchants who worked in America. By the late 1990s, Abdou told me, the number of West African art traders working in North America had grown by leaps and bounds.

Abdou suggested two reasons for the expansion. He said that

people now thought that "wood" qualified as important art. This new appreciation attracted new groups of collectors who wanted to invest in art objects the values of which would quickly increase. At the time, Abdou had a long list of private collectors. They would contact him about what they wanted, and he or one of his colleagues would try to find and deliver the object. Abdou also mentioned the increased African American interest in African objects. He said that African American shoppers liked to buy kente cloth strips and hats from West African street vendors in Harlem. Eventually, he said, this interest prompted an increasing number of African American collectors to visit his stall at the Warehouse.

: : :

A variety of cultural and economic forces created the perfect context for the expansion of the African art trade in North America. By the early 1990s scores of traders in masks, figurines—wooden, iron, and terra-cotta—antique weapons, and cloth had made their way to New York City. Together they formed the Warehouse community of West African merchants.

3 ::: NEW YORK CITY AND
TRANSNATIONAL TRADE

A cold January morning in 2001—loading day at the Warehouse. Scores of Ford Econoline vans, the West African art traders transport vehicle of choice, were backed up against the Warehouse's loading docks. Clusters of young men, dressed in down—or ersatz down—coats loaded a wide variety to West and Central African objects into the vans: Guro masks and Baule "colonial" figurines from Côte d'Ivoire, two statues of Dogon ancestors from Mali, several large pieces of handwoven kente cloth and a collection of wooden stools from Ghana, and a bundle of raffia mats and a cache of iron weapons from Congo.

Amid the throng I saw Idrissa Soumana, a Songhay man from Fillingue, which is just north of El Hajj Yaya's hometown of Belayara. Idrissa is known as "the chauffeur," a man who ceaselessly drives shipments of African art all over the United States—from trade show to trade show from city to city, from the Northeast to the Southwest. In his time in America Idrissa says that he's been to every state in his white Econoline van. Although he has lived in Harlem in New York City, he has spent most of his time driving the interstates and sleeping in cheap motels.

"Paul," Idrissa said, "I want you to meet my friend, Gugul."

"Gugul?" I ask.

"He's the art doctor. His real name is Ag Gugul Ibegart."

I followed Idrissa through a series of dimly lit corridors to a small musty room in which a ceiling light illuminated stacks of broken statues and cracked masks. Gugul sat on a metal chair, gluing the severed arm of a figurine to its torso. He wore jeans, a loose-fitting gray shirt, and a New York Yankees baseball cap.

I greeted Gugul in Songhay.

He looked at me and smiled. "Which planet did you drop in from?"

I mentioned that I had heard he came from Gorom-Gorom, a small sandy and windswept village in far northeast Burkina Faso near the Nigerien border.

"Have you been to Gorom-Gorom?" he asked.

"No, but I've been to Wanzerbe and Markoye," I countered, mentioning villages proximate to Gorom-Gorom. "I spent a lot of time in Mehanna," I mentioned.

"I know Mehanna," he said. "I used to do a market circuit: Gorom-Gorom, Markoye, Wanzerbe, and Mehanna," he said. "Mehanna was the biggest of them all."

"Even in the absence of food," I said, invoking a Songhay idiom, "Mehanna is sweet."

"That's the truth," Gugul said, smiling broadly. He was a lean man with a face set into a serious expression. "What are you doing here?" he asked.

I explained to him my New York City project on art. I told him El Hajj Yaya had been teaching me about the art trade. "Before that, I spent several years with the Harlem merchants."

"I've been in New York for seven years," he said. "I live in Brooklyn."

"How did you become the art doctor?"

"When I cam here, I befriended Mounmouni, the previous art doctor, also from Gorom-Gorom. He taught me."

"So you've been doing repairs for a long time."

"Too long. My work never ends," he sighed. "I'm tired and I miss home," he continued, echoing a sentiment that Yaya and his brothers often expressed. "Soon I'll return to Gorom-Gorom."

I looked at the array of broken masks and figurines.

"They don't pack the objects very well," Gugul said. "Many of them break in transit and I put them back together."

"So this is where you do all your repairs?"

Gugul shakes his head. "I have another workshop. Want to see it?"

Idrissa, Gugul, and I wandered through the corridors, finally finding an exit to Twenty-Eighth Street. Gugul led us east toward Tenth Avenue. As snow flurries swirled in the gusty wind coming off the Hudson River, we crossed the street. We descended a trash-strewn stairwell leading to a black metal door. Gugul opened it, revealing a dim and dank basement filled with broken art scattered here and there. On a long table Gugul had arranged various cans of Minwax and glue among a variety of screwdrivers, hammers, needle-nosed and flat-nosed pliers, gouging tools, paintbrushes, and sanding blocks.

"I want to open my own business—be more independent," Gugul said. "If that works, I'll make more money. That way I'll be able to go home sooner."

"What about your space at the Warehouse?" I asked.

"I'm training a man from Burkina. When he's ready he'll take over."[1]

⋮ ⋮ ⋮

In 2002, Ousmane Zongo, Gugul's replacement who, like the Art Doctor, came from Burkina Faso, began to do repair work at the Warehouse. Unlike Gugul, he spoke little, if any, English and hadn't a clue about American culture. In the spring of 2003, his lack of cultural competence and the gross negligence of the New York City Police Department (NYPD) cost him his life. Responding to the trial of the NYPD officers responsible for Ousmane Zongo's death, Dan Barry, a *New York Times* columnist who writes about life in the city, reconstructed what happened to the luckless art doctor.

Two men alone: one black, one white, from vastly different cultures. And only one would live to tell his version of their clash.

Officer Conroy did not greet the man; he did not play it cool. He later told a grand jury that, alone and dressed as a mail carrier, he felt vulnerable. That, he said, is why he pulled his handgun as he repeatedly identified himself as a police officer.

In the officer's testimony, Mr. Zongo's response seems both menacing and Christ like. He walked slowly toward the pointed gun, Officer Conroy said, hands at his sides, palms outward, head lowered—then lunged before turning and running away. The officer chased him down the storage facility's weird corridors, shouting "1085" into his radio: Officer in pursuit; backup requested.

At the end of a corridor, Officer Conroy said later, Mr. Zongo went for the gun. In the ensuing struggle, he said, he managed to pull back and shoot five times. Then he sent another radio message, a "1013": Officer needs assistance right away. And call an ambulance.[2]

Ousmane Zongo died unarmed—a needless death. The NYPD had failed to train Officer Conroy sufficiently—an unnecessary killing.

The shocking death of Ousmane Zongo sapped the once-vibrant life of the Warehouse. Wishing to leave a space of death, many art traders began to store their wares in other, less tainted facilities. Several traders moved to Atlanta, Houston, and Chicago. Older traders returned to Mali, Senegal, and Niger. Eventually, the owners of Chelsea Mini Storage raised the rental rates on ground-floor space, which pushed the remaining traders out of the building. In an ironic turnaround, high-end galleries, seeking some of the limelight of the emerging Chelsea art scene, took over the ground floor of Chelsea Mini Storage, transforming it from third world to first world space.

The new Warehouse is hard to recognize. Gone is the first floor mosque, the meeting room with junkyard furniture. Gone is the "African" kitchen, from which aromatic odors mixed with the ever-present scent of wood smoke. Gone are the showrooms of African traders featuring the arts and crafts of West, Central, and East Africa. Traders still cluster in front of the Warehouse's two entrances. If you engage them, they'll get you a visitor's pass, take you to the elevator, and then lead you through the dim hallways to lockers stocked with African art.

"It was better in the days before," one Malian trader told me. "We're still here, but many of my brothers have left."

: : :

The economic slowdown brought on by the aftermath of 9/11 and a growing distrust of Muslims convinced many traders to leave the trading life in African art. In some cases, these events compelled traders to become itinerant merchants, always on the move among North America, Europe, Asia, and West Africa.

One such merchant is Angu Sandi, a trader from Niger whom I met when he initially came to New York City in 1994. Angu Sandi's story adds a new dimension to the Eagles' hit song "Life in the Fast Lane." The lyrics of the song tell the story of a couple who race through life, doing drugs that enable them, or so they think, to live life to its limits. They take many foolish risks to be on life's cutting edge. Eventually, they seek thrills at such great speeds that they lose control of their lives as well as their car, which goes so fast they can't negotiate a curve in the road. They go over a cliff and crash.

Like the couple in the song, Angu has been a risk taker, but his gambles have been calculated—never foolish. He hasn't needed to seek the cutting edge of life, for his creative economic maneuvers have put him squarely on the fast lane of contemporary transnational trade.

: : :

When I traveled to Niger in February 2009, I reconnected with Angu. Before traveling to Niger that winter I went to the Malcolm Shabazz Harlem Market to visit my friends and procure some last minute information. My friends gave me Moussa Boureima's cell phone number. He had returned to Niger the previous year.

The morning after my arrival, I telephoned Moussa Boureima from my hotel room. I was immediately connected, but a great deal of background noise complicated our conversation.

"Moussa. Moussa. It's Paul. I'm in Niamey."

"God be praised," he replied, but given the background noise, I could hardly hear him. "Did you arrive in good health?"

"I did," I replied. "Where are you?"

"In the bush; I'm walking my fields." There was a momentary silence. "There's a lot of wind today."

In New York City Moussa Boureima seemed like a big, thick, and reticent man. In Niger, his distant voice sounded strong and sure. I imagined him striding confidently through his fields, his cell phone pushed against his ear. Getting a grip, I asked if he had Angu Sandi's telephone number. Angu had been Moussa's roommate in the South Bronx.

"I do," he replied. "Let me look it up on my contact list."

Moments later, I had the number and telephoned Angu.

"It is not true. Monsieur Paul in Niamey," Angu said in his peculiar version of English.

"I'm at the Grand Hotel."

"Grand Hotel? Don't move. I'm coming for you."

Thirty minutes later, I walked into the lobby of the Grand Hotel and looked for my friend, but recognized no one. Suddenly two men stood up and walked toward me.

"Paul, you don't recognize me," Angu said.

He was dressed in a long damask gold shirt embroidered with intricate geometric patterns that covered a matching set of trousers. A stringy white goatee lengthened his chin. On what I remembered to have been a bald head he wore a gold kufi fashioned from silk. Angu was thinner and apparently much more prosperous than my frozen-in-time New York City image of him. In fact, he looked younger than the man I had met fifteen years earlier. "You look fit," I said.

"I am well," he said giving me a hug. He then introduced his younger brother, Ali, a short, powerfully built man whose white robes and white kufi contrasted strikingly with his black skin. "Paul, Angu has told me so much about you."

"Were you with Angu in New York?" I asked.

"Yes."

Although Angu said that Ali was his younger brother, I later found out that they were, in fact, cousins.

Angu grabbed my hand. "Paul, let's go. I've got my car here."

We popped into Angu's 2000 Honda Accord, which he had purchased at a car auction in North Carolina. After a transatlantic voyage in a container and a long drive from the port city of Cotonou, Benin, it finally arrived in Niamey.

"Honda is good," Angu said as he turned the ignition. "No trouble. But this one doesn't have air-conditioning. This year, I'll get a new car from America—with air-conditioning."

The absence of a breeze made the midday Sahelian heat intense. We drove through Niamey's cluttered streets: donkey-pulled carts filled with cartons of goods, motorcyclists wearing face masks—protection from the dust. A parade of beggars flowed through the streets. Blind men and women held on to the hands of children. Polio victims made their way on hand-propelled bicycles. Somehow the beggars maneuvered around fast-moving trucks overloaded with grain. We left the paved road and wandered through a maze of sandy byways lined with shops, their doors and windows open, their goods on display. We parked the car next to Hamidou's peanut oil shop and rolled a tarp over the car. "I know Hamidou," Angu said. "He makes sure no one messes with my car."

After walking a few meters from Hamidou's we turned right onto a sandy path that led toward the Grand Marché. Everyone seemed to know Angu. We stopped a dozen times and greeted Angu's colleagues and friends.

"This is my friend Paul. I knew him in New York and now he's come to Niger."

Everyone raised both arms skyward and gave thanks to God.

"Your friend," one man said to me, "has become a big man—very rich, very admired."

A tall thick man grabbed my hands. "Paul, don't you remember me?"

I didn't recognize him.

"We met in New York. I went there a year ago. We talked in Harlem."

"Oh yes. You are one of the New Yorkais."

The man beamed with delight. "That's right," he said acknowledging the title Nigeriens give to men who have returned from an economic sojourn in New York City.

We finally made it to the Avenue de la Liberté, one of Niamey's main thoroughfares, beyond which lay the Grande Marché, a huge square space that comprises several city blocks. The avenue was clogged with shoppers, donkeys, and street vendors hawking their wares. On the side of the road, men loaded and unloaded dozens of trucks.

We wove our way through the throng and entered the market. The narrow passageways, protected from the sun by tent cloth attached to the roofs of the stalls, led us deep into the market. We finally came to Angu's small space, situated at the corner of two passageways. He had stuffed his shop with textiles and carpets from Dubai and Songhay and Hausa blankets. Three card-table

FIGURE 7. Angu Sandi in his shop, Grande Marché, Niamey, Niger,
February 2009. Photo by the author.

chairs stood opened and unoccupied on the floor. Two oscillat-
ing fans blew relatively cool air onto our hot bodies.

As soon as we sat down, well-wishers poured in to greet the
guest from New York. I met Angu's cousins, his younger brother,
and four of his sons, all of whom worked for him. A stream of
his business associates popped in to pay their respects. One man
proposed a $10,000 sale of Nigerien blankets and Libyan carpets.
Angu agreed to the sale and told the man to come back later in
the day—to arrange delivery and payment. Just then Angu took
a phone call.

"Yes El Hajj, I know. When will you make the shipment?
Tomorrow is good."

He turned to me. "That's my friend in Germany. We do good
business," Angu said, smiling. As he was talking with his part-

ner in Frankfurt, Germany, two teenagers delivered six pieces of canvas luggage. Phone in hand, Angu signaled for them to stack the bags outside the entrance to the shop. Still bantering with his friend in Germany, he reached into his pocket and pulled out a huge wad of African francs and paid the boys. He then nonchalantly finished his international conversation.

A Hausa butcher came with a plate of roasted meat—beef fillet. Angu asked him to cut up some pieces, which he did, putting the morsels on a small plate. "Taste it," he said to me.

"It's delicious," I said, savoring a juicy chunk. I asked Angu when he would next go to America to buy cars.

"You know it's been nine months since I was there. I bought cars in Harrisburg and Greensboro. Good prices. But when the cars went to Cotonou, there weren't many buyers. Those cars sat on the docks for months. That's not good business. The market is not good right now."

"You're talking about the recession in the United States?"

"Business is bad everywhere. People aren't buying." Reflecting upon the devaluation of African currencies, Angu said, "They lowered the value of the Nigerian naira." He shook his head. "My Nigerian friends can't buy cars right now." He moved toward a desk he had squeezed into the corner of a congested shop. He opened the desk drawer. "I want to show you something."

He pulled out a packet and threw it my lap.

"What's this?" I asked incredulously.

"There's $9,999 in that bundle."

"Why do you have so much cash here?"

"I'll use it the next time I go to America."

"But don't you have a bank account?"

"Sure," he said, taking out his checkbook. "Sure I do."

He then opened an envelope and showed me the business cards of his American associates—bankers, automobile parts dealers, car detailers, mechanics, transatlantic shipping agents, car auction brokers, lawyers, and shipping insurance agents who provided professional services in Pennsylvania, New York, New Jersey, Maryland, Virginia, North Carolina, Georgia, and Florida. "These are my friends in America," Angu said.

Angu's phone rang once again. He spoke rapidly in Hausa. I could catch a few words of the conversation, including the word "kuti," which in Hausa means "money." The call didn't last very long. "That was my little brother in Greensboro. He says hello and wishes you a good time in Niger."

Another cousin joined Ali, Angu, and me in the shop. We launched into a discussion of American politics. They wondered about Barack Obama.

"Imagine," Angu said, "a black man is president of the United States. America is back," he said.

"Do you think he will make it better over there," Ali asked, "so we can go there again and do business?"

"I don't know," I admitted.

The muezzin called the faithful to early afternoon prayer. My friends went to the Grand Marché mosque. "After prayers, we'll go to eat," Angu told me.

I talked with Angu's sons about life in United States. Two of their brothers live in West Palm Beach, Florida, where they do odd jobs. Angu's sons in Niamey, both in their early twenties, wanted to go to the United States.

"We have no work here," one of them said, "I'm an accountant, but I can't get work. So I work with my father. Last year, I tried to find my way to America, but I couldn't get a visa. Can you help me?"

I explained that I didn't work for the embassy and that my recommendation would have no bearing on who might—or might not—get a visa. They also told me that Nigeriens didn't immigrate to France all that much. "Nigeriens don't like the French," said Moctar, the second oldest of Angu's four sons.

When the shop phone rang, Moctar answered it. "That's Baba. I'll walk you to his car." I followed Moctar down a slimy passageway, greeting merchants along the way. The stench of urine assailed us at the public toilet. Moving our way quickly past the latrine, we emerged into bright sunlight. Dodging donkey carts, boys hawking phone cards and sunglasses, and impatient taxi drivers, I crossed the Avenue de la Liberté and joined Angu and his "little brother," Ali, who sometimes traveled with him in the United States. We drove down the clogged streets toward our destination, an African restaurant. Ali began to criticize Angu's driving. Angu shot back that his younger brother knew nothing about anything. They slapped each other on the shoulder and laughed, enjoying the dynamics of their joking relationship.

"In the United States you two drove ten hours in the same car?" I wondered. "It's not possible."

Laughter exploded in the car as we turned left, toward the east and Angu's neighborhood. Along the sandy edge of the road piles of garbage lay rotting in the intense sunlight, giving off a nose-crinkling stench. Mixed among the mud-brick houses we passed was an assortment of businesses—a laundry and dry-cleaning shop, a telephone recharging shop. Amid scores of bicycle wheels and tires, a young man repaired a gearshift. In the shade of a scraggly acacia, another young man repaired an automobile tire. Men sat behind shaded tables where they sold cigarettes, kola, chewing gum, and batteries. A woman emerged from an opening in the wall and dumped a basin of soapy water onto the sand. We finally came to our cross street, which was paved, and turned right. In the distance we saw our destination, marked by a hand-painted sign, "African Restaurant—Plats Delicieux," which was fastened to the roof of a hangar. After parking the car in the shade, we walked under the hangar—shady but still hot. Four tables, covered with cotton cloth and surrounded by green plastic chairs, had been arranged at one end of the rectangular space. At the other end, six big pots—one for rice, one for couscous, and one for *fufu* (cassava paste), and three for chicken, meat, and fish sauce, had been placed on a long table. A large woman with a round face sat at a desk next to a cash box—the owner and cook.

The owner directed us to a table in the corner. We sat next to three stout men dressed in long damask shirts that covered matching damask trousers—the Sahelian business suit. Angu knew one of them, whom he greeted. As we sat down, one gentleman proposed a $500 trade. Angu accepted and arranged to meet his associate later in the afternoon.

The owner brought us food—chicken, carrots, and cabbage in a zesty sauce for me; fish, carrots, and cabbage for Angu; and couscous, beef, and vegetables for Ali. She also brought us Coca-Colas. As is the custom, we ate, but did not engage in conversation. A chirping cell phone soon disturbed the silence of eating. Angu answered and spoke in Songhay for several minutes.

"That's my friend whose shop is across from mine. He's calling from Bamako. We like to do deals."

Before we had finished eating, another phone called disrupted us. This one, it turned out, was from a business associate in Dubai. Angu said he planned to go there sometime in March or April to buy cloth and carpets.

Our delicious meal finally completed, we drove to Yantala, a neighborhood on Niamey's north side. "We have to go and see some people," Angu announced.

Driving through narrow sandy paths encased by the walls of mud-brick compounds, we meandered through the frenzied and cluttered life of Niamey—children playing near heaps of garbage or in puddles of discarded wash water, men sleeping in chairs shaded by acacia trees, herds of goats rummaging for scraps of food, boys unloading large sacks of grain from large trucks, young men zigzagging through the dusty byways on their motorcycles. At our destination, I saw a group of men sitting on palm frond mats that had been unrolled under a hangar.

"Is this a funeral?" I asked.

"Yes," Angu said. "My third wife's father."

We paid our respects to the assembled men and walked into the compound to greet the women. *Fo nda tilas* is a greeting that means "that which is necessary—death," which awaits us all.

Angu's father-in-law, who was seventy-five years old, died suddenly the previous evening. Meeting his familial obligations, Angu made time to spend with his in-laws.

In the shade of the hangar, we talked very little about the life of the deceased, but did discuss the economic downturn, market conditions, the price of gasoline, and the unusual heat for early February. Sensing the visible fatigue of his American friend, Angu offered to drop me off.

He smiled: "My day is just beginning."

: : :

Like most all of his West African compatriots who live the trading life, Angu is strategically situated in a series of social and economic networks. This intense emphasis on social relations, I think, stems in part from a West African notion of prosperity. In West Africa there are two conceptions of wealth. There is tangible wealth that is expressed in money, houses, clothing, and cars. But there is also an intangible kind of wealth that is expressed in the extent and complexity of personal networks—wealth in people. Individuals in the world who enjoy both kinds of wealth are truly prosperous, and in West Africa at least are very much admired.

There are some West Africans, however, who, despite their wealth in money, have few if any people they can count on in their networks. Although most West Africans would want to enjoy such tangible wealth, they would feel sorry for the wealthy person who walks alone. Finally, there are people who lack substantial financial resources but work hard to maintain large networks of people upon whom they can depend for housing, food, and financial help. It is an obligation that, for better or worse, places a social and financial burden on those who have both wealth in money and wealth in people. And yet it is a burden willingly accepted by most of the merchants I've come to know during the past thirty years. It is a burden that brings them social prestige.

But the business of social relations is not a one-way street. The wealthy may empty their wallets to those in their networks who are old or sick or simply lazy, but the old, the sick, and even the lazy know that in return they must give back. They pay homage to their benefactors, singing their praises and spreading the word of their "selfless" generosity. It takes two hands, as the Songhay saying goes, to build a friendship, to establish and maintain one's connection in a network.

: : :

The study of networks and social relations is nothing new in the human sciences. In anthropology the study of social relations has a long history, beginning with the description of kindreds and kin-related networks and continuing on through the analysis of social networks. The anthropological study of networks first focused on personal ties. Who is connected to the network's central figure? How intense is the contact of the central figure to various people in her or his configuration? These preliminary studies developed into the more abstract—and mathematically sophisticated—study of whole networks that one is more likely to find in the literatures of sociology and social psychology. Here scholars are less interested in the business of social relations and more concerned with the multidimensional dynamics that lead to phenomena like six degrees of separation.[3] Some of this work sparked the curiosity of mathematicians and physicists interested in self-adapting complex systems, which led to theoretical work on chaos theory, connective hubs, and, my favorite, the edge of chaos, the perfect storm of self-adapting systems.[4] The key to this fascinating work, which is primarily based upon mathematical simulations of complex relations, is to find elegantly simple principles that organize what appears to be a chaotic sequence of events. I have much admiration for the scholars whose work has given us deep insights into the murky worlds of complex (social) relations. The world of social relations, however, at least in my experience of it, is always more convoluted than the most complex multidimensional simulations.

Angu's network is a case in point. He is linked to paternal and maternal relations, both blood kin and affines, through social obligation and economic ties. These same social obligations and economic links connect him to friends from his village, Dogondoutchi, as well as other Hausa-speaking merchants who hail from his region of Niger. He has blood kin in several key cities on the East Coast of the United States. Two sons live in south Florida, where they can help facilitate the shipment of used cars, usually Hondas and Toyotas, from the Florida coast to the port of Cotonou on the Bight of Benin in West Africa.[5] He has two paternal cousins who live in Greensboro, North Carolina, the location of a large population of immigrants from Niger. Greensboro is near important used car auction sites in Charlotte, North Carolina, and Richmond, Virginia. Angu also has compatriots, all of whom are Hausa from his region of Niger, who live in New York City. They sometimes travel with him or for him to Harrisburg, Pennsylvania, the site of another substantial used car auction. They make contact with American bonding agents so that they can purchase the vehicles; American detailers, who clean the cars to almost mint condition; and American shipping agents, who put the Africa-bound vehicles on cargo boats in Baltimore. In Cotonou, Angu is networked with compatriots, again Hausa men from his region, who sell the cars. After taking their modest commission, they transfer funds to Angu's bank accounts.

Through transnational connections of people, goods, and money, Angu has become a wealthy man in the true African sense of the term. He has very healthy bank accounts in dollars, euros, and West African francs. He has a substantial number of associates in his transnational networks. He takes care of them and they look after him—the very definition of West African wealth and well-being.

: : :

During an October 2000 interview at the Warehouse, Yaya talked at length about his colleague and compatriot Angu. He also described the general business climate for African traders. Yaya and his brothers, unlike Angu, avoided the used car business, which they found too risky. Yaya mentioned Angu's early difficulties. Before Angu ventured to the United States to buy used cars, he and his partner would fly from Niger to Germany, buy two Mercedes sedans, and drive them to Marseille. From Marseille they'd take a ferry to Oran or Algiers, join a car caravan, and cross the Sahara. When they eventually arrived in Niger, they could sell the vehicle for two to three times what they paid. But used car traders, Yaya suggested, faced considered risks and costs. Along the Saharan route bandits would steal cars and loot them for their lucrative parts. If you managed to avoid vehicle theft, you still had to pay import taxes, border crossing fees, and the ever-present "dash" to customs officers. Sometimes these bribes, Yaya explained, could be quite high, which, of course, reduced considerably a person's margin of profit.

"But wouldn't it be less risky to transport used cars from America to West Africa?"

"Yes, but there are so many steps and costs," he told me during the same October 2000 interview. He went on to explain how traders like Angu had to pay fees to used car brokers, detailers, and international shipping firms. "The costs are high," he said, "and after all that work, the car could be damaged during transport. Even if you have insurance, you would not recover your costs."

Yaya and his brothers opted to remain in the African art business. For them the sale of "wood" and "mud" would bring considerable profits they could reinvest in additional masks and statuettes. Yaya and his brothers also used the proceeds of their North American sales to purchase diamonds and rubies, build new houses in Abidjan and their hometown of Belayara, or buy transport vehicles. "Besides," as Yaya would often say, "I really like the art. I like it when these objects surround me."

Time, however, took a toll on Yaya's family. Late in 1998, Yaya's older brother, Abdou, became ill. Distrust of and perceived lack of access to American medical care convinced him to try his luck, first in Côte d'Ivoire and then back home in Niger. He received treatment for his "sickness," but he eventually died in 1999 at the age of seventy.

When Yaya gave me the horrible news of Abdou's death, I asked what had happened to his older brother.

"He got sick and died."

Yaya did not want to talk about it.

"We leave the dead in peace," he told me. "It was his time."

Yaya still had his younger brother, Daouda, who would come to New York when he was conducting business in West Africa. Prior to our early October 2000 meeting at the Warehouse, Yaya had spent roughly eighteen months in Niger, where he had begun to build a collection of antique pottery and terra-cotta figurines and pots. He began to acquire these objects in 1995. By the time he had arrived in New York City in late summer of 2000, he had amassed a substantial collection of antique items from Niger and Burkina Faso. Indeed, the collection of reliquary terra-cotta figures from Bura, Niger, he told me proudly, now filled an entire storage locker at the Warehouse.

During our conversation Yaya filled in some details of his personal life. He had two wives, both of whom lived in Niamey, Niger. His family now included ten children and two grandchildren.

FIGURE 8. Bura reliquary figurine. Photo by the author.

"What are the names of your wives?" I asked.

"We don't talk much about our wives or our young children. It's bad luck."

He did mention that he wanted his oldest son, who was at the time twenty-four years old, to come to America, where Yaya would introduce him to the art and teach him the essentials of long-distance trade. That way Yaya could trust the business to his son and return to his wives and children who lived rather comfortably in a spacious Niamey villa. "I miss my family and want to spend more time at home."

Yaya told me that since he began to trade in America in 1991, his business had prospered. Early in his American experience, he traveled to Los Angeles; Minneapolis; Philadelphia; Washington, DC; Atlanta; Houston; San Francisco; and Chicago. In those early years, he sold Tuareg silver jewelry (tooled rings, the aforementioned Croix d'Agadez necklace, various West African masks and statuettes, and leather sandals and boxes covered with tooled leather—the latter being the work of Tuareg smiths from the Belayara region.[6]

Two weeks later I once again visited the Warehouse, which, as usual, abounded with commercial activity. Scores of Econoline vans had been backed up to the loading docks. Young men piled a motley assortment of masks and statuettes on the loading bays—objects that would be put into the vans that would carry the cargo to Washington, DC, Chicago; Atlanta; Indianapolis; New Orleans; Dallas; and Houston. The pieces I saw looked new, poorly crafted, and recently painted—tourist art. I entered the Warehouse and found Yaya seated in front of his stall on the first floor near the Warehouse's prayer room. We talked at length about the market for African art. He said that market had been good, mentioning that most of his colleagues would easily exhaust their inventories well before the expiration of their six-month business visas.

I mentioned the tourist pieces I had seen on my way in.

"If you have new pieces, you shouldn't sell them to good clients unless they really want them. It's best to take new pieces to Chicago and other places where there are festivals."

Like most of his colleagues, Yaya had a deep knowledge of both the aesthetics and economics of the African art market. As it was harvest time in Niger, I asked him about agricultural conditions in West Africa. The harvest looked like it would be a spotty, he admitted, but his sons had carefully looked after the fields and expected a decent harvest of millet and sorghum. "My family will be fine," he said.

Yaya then invited me to see his collection of Bura terra-cotta reliquary figurines.

"We need to go upstairs," he announced.

I followed Yaya through the twists and turns of the dimly lit first floor. We entered the office of Chelsea Mini Storage, where a manager gave us two badges that would get us on the freight elevator—an antique machine replete with folding steel mesh, an operating lever, and an operator, a young Hispanic man who inspected our badges. "Which floor, gentlemen?"

The operator took us to the fifth floor. We exited and I followed Yaya into a dank and dark grid of relatively narrow corridors bordered by storage lockers. We came upon an open locker. Its owner, a West African art trader from Mali, had removed several Bamana and Dogon masks. In the dim light, we couldn't see if the pieces might be in need of repair.

"How much will you pay for the Dogon monkey mask?" he asked me in French.

"I'm not buying today," I responded.

"I need money," he said. "You pay $75 for the monkey mask— a very good deal."

"It is," I said, "but I'm really not buying."

True to form, the trader did not buy my "not buying" response. "You can take it for $65. Take it. I'll lose money, but take it."

Yaya interjected. "He's with me." That ended the conversation.

Yaya took me to the north end of the Warehouse. From his deep pocket he removed a key and a flashlight. He opened his padlocked door and shone the light on a room full of Bura reliquary figurines. There must have been fifty to seventy-five objects staring back at me—hauntingly.

To be honest, the sight of this collection triggered deep-seated ethical concerns. Frankly, I wondered how he had obtained these old pieces. More troubling still, I had recently read that Nigerien archaeologist Boube Gado had condemned the looting of the Bura site he had excavated in 1983. I also discovered that in 1997, the International Council of Museums (ICOM) published their Red List of plundered archaeological objects, a list that included reliquaries from the Bura civilization in southwest Niger and eastern Burkina Faso. According to the Red List report:

> Scientific excavations carried out since 1983 by the *Institut de recherches en sciences humaines* (I.R.S.H.) in Niger brought to light the so-called Bura objects. These are large terracotta funeral jars, which may be tubular or ovoid in shape, topped by heads, effigies or even horsemen. Also from this region are the stone sculptures now available on the art market, a few examples only of which were found during official excavations.
>
> The heads of these figurines are generally flat, rectangular or oblong in shape. A large number are scarified, and the busts are often crisscrossed with intertwined pearl-strung shoulder-bands carrying quivers and weapons. Bracelets have been added to the arms. The jars on which these statuettes were fixed are decorated with incisions. Some jars form the body itself of the figurines, the upper limbs being represented in relief.
>
> The rigorous methods used in excavation work, both at the surface and in stratigraphic analysis, have enabled information on burials in the Bura system from the 2nd

to the 11th centuries to be gathered. It throws light on the meaning of the statues and the particular functions of each site.

But, once the existence of these ancient cultures became public knowledge, particularly in Western countries, wide-scale looting ensued. A whole network for the illegal export of objects, using neighboring countries among others as channels, has resulted in the massive loss of sculptures. On the Western art market, these have sometimes been "identified" as being from Mali or Burkina Faso. Archaeologists are very alarmed, as all the archaeological sites in the region are systematically looted, and the information contained in these sites is destroyed.[7]

Yaya looked at me looking at the locker filled with haunting terra-cotta reliquaries—simply magnificent pieces.

"These belong in a museum," I suggested, rather defensively.

Yaya nodded. "They're fine and old pieces. I've had them carbon-14 tested."

I registered my naive surprise. "I see."

"You've got to get them tested to verify the age," he stated in a matter-of-fact way.

"What were the results?"

"Some of the best pieces are around one thousand years old. The tests aren't exact."

"So I've heard."

"Since getting the pieces, their value has gone up."

"Do you have a lot of buyers?"

"In the past, yes, but no so many these days."

"How did you collect these pieces?" I asked.

Yaya did not hesitate. When he heard about the Bura excavation, he quickly realized the economic potential of the objects. He hired a truck and crew to go to the site, which, during the early years, was unprotected. He then supervised the extraction of objects. More recently, he said, it had been too risky for him to go to Bura. "There's a law protecting the objects," he said. "Soldiers are protecting the site."

"Did you stop collecting them at that time?" I asked.

"No. I hired local people to dig up the objects and bring them to me for a good price. They need money. So even though there are soldiers, they dig up the pieces and bring them to the local market."

I told him why I had problems with this kind of collecting. "When you just dig them up, you destroy the site, which means you can no longer study the past."

"Yes, but people in Bura are very poor," he responded. "They need money, and finding the objects is a way for them to get money."

"Don't you think they should be in the museum in Niamey?"

"There are many pieces in the museum already," he said. "People like old and beautiful pieces."

"Well, Yaya, I disagree."

He shrugged. "We have different ideas about it. It doesn't matter, I'm not going to collect any more of these Buras—too difficult to get them and even more difficult to sell."

"So what will you do with them?"

"I'll sell them to private clients and to galleries. That will be the end of it. Now I want to sell Tuareg jewelry and Tuareg writing drawn on rocks and hard wood."

"Petrified wood?"

"That's it," he said slapping me on the back. "I'll be getting some of those soon. When you come back, you'll see them." [8]

: : :

Shortly after my introduction to the haunting Bura reliquaries imprisoned in a storage locker on the fifth floor of the Warehouse, Yaya left New York City for a long period of time. After Yaya's departure, the American people elected George W. Bush to the presidency of the United States. Indeed, many of Yaya's West African colleagues compared the contested vote count in Florida to the highly corrupt and highly familiar—to them at least—electoral practices that unfold in West African nations. When 9/11 occurred, Yaya was in Niamey, Niger's capital, tending to his various enterprises. In the wake of 9/11, the West African community in New York City suffered profoundly. My friends at the Malcolm Shabazz Harlem Market and those at the Warehouse experienced a significant business slowdown. My friends said that Americans did not want to spend money on African art or on anything else—especially in New York City, the site of the terrorist attack. West African traders at the Warehouse and at the Harlem market, most of whom were Muslim, also claimed that as a result of 9/11, Americans hated all Muslims—even those who hailed from sub-Saharan Africa.

They don't like it when we pray or when we wear African robes, Boube Mounkaila told me in the summer of 2002. That reminds them of the attacks. He suggested that the combination of the post-9/11 economic downturn and Islamophobia had diminished substantially the West African immigrant's quality of life in America. Many of the traders became mobile merchants, traveling from trade show to trade show in search of sales and dwindling profits.

Ensconced in Belayara and Niamey, Yaya did not suffer economically during this period. In fact, he decided to invest more heavily in Tuareg silver jewelry, which he could buy easily and cheaply. These small items were easy to transport and were not subject, like textiles, to a customs duty. In addition, he could price them reasonably, which would assure quick sales and good profits. From Niger he began to ship cartons of Tuareg necklaces, rings, and sheathed daggers to his colleagues at the Malcolm Shabazz Harlem Market in New York City.

In phone conversations, Yaya said that he would not return to the United States until the autumn of 2002. He liked being in Niger. What's more, given the economic slowdown, he didn't want to spend a great deal of time in North America. Indeed, he hadn't been able to sell many of the terra-cotta reliquaries he had showed me during our last visit together. I asked him what he intended to do. He said that he would reduce his prices for the remaining terra-cotta figures but hold on to the figurines with intricate designs.

He also found that the bad economy had created many conflicts in the West African trading community in New York, which meant that he wanted to limit his next visit to one month. That month would give him time to train one of his blood relatives. That relative, he told me, would eventually receive shipments of Tuareg silver jewelry and sell the pieces to large department stores, galleries of African art, or to small boutiques. His replacement would also contact Yaya's long list of private clients, who would be interested in collecting reasonably priced antique silver.

True to his word, Yaya spent only one month in New York and returned to Niger in early November 2002. He remained there for two years. Periodically, he would phone our friends at the Malcolm Shabazz Harlem Market and through them pass along to me his greetings from Niamey and Belayara. When I visited New York, I missed our conversations about the aesthetics of African art, stories of his pilgrimage to Mecca, and discussions of the role of Islam in economic practices. But I sensed that he was quite pleased to be at home in Niger with his family.

TWO

A LIFE STORY IN ANTHROPOLOGY

4 ::: SILVER SPRING

My beginnings could not have been more different from those of Yaya. Unlike the young Yaya who lived in Belayara, Niger, in a small mud-brick house that lacked running water and interior plumbing, I spent my childhood and adolescence in a modest three-bedroom house in a middle-class neighborhood of Silver Spring, Maryland, which is a close-in suburb of Washington, DC. We had a bathroom, a powder room, a basement, and lots of space in a grassy backyard where I played with my childhood friends.

My parents, Sidney Stoller and Goldie Berman, came from thoroughly Jewish households. My great-grandfather, Joe Stoller, was a carpenter who built and repaired houses in small villages in Belorussia. He trained his son, Mack, in the trade. But the early years of the twentieth century brought turmoil to Belorussia—especially for Jews. Seeking refuge from Cossack pogroms and from eventual conscription into the czar's World War I army, father and son slipped out of Belorussia and landed in Windsor, Canada. They eventually made their way across Lake Erie and established themselves in Detroit, where, when resources permitted, they brought over other members of the family.

My grandfather, Mack Stoller, married Rose Swartz, the oldest child of the inimitable Swartz family. They had three children: my father Sidney, Raymond, and Beverly. My father was born in Detroit in 1920. A few years later the family moved to Washington, DC, where some of their landsmen (people from the same village) had settled. At that time, Washington, DC, seemed to be a city of limitless opportunity. My grandfather left the bulk of the

FIGURE 9. Mack Stoller becomes an American citizen, circa 1919.

FIGURE 10.
Sidney Stoller
heads to the
Pacific, 1943.

family, including my great-grandfather, back in Detroit, where
Joe Stoller had a modest business. My grandfather used his meager savings to open a small grocery store in southwest Washington, DC. The store was not a great success. Struggling in the grocery business, my grandfather's landsmen encouraged him to go
into the building business. Working hard in a trade that he had
known since childhood, he made enough money to provide my
father and his siblings with a comfortable home and a relatively
prosperous life. In 1938 my father and his brother, Raymond,
shared a car—with a rumble seat no less!

My father attended law school but did not find the law to
his liking. As World War II unfolded he and his brother joined

FIGURE 11.

Goldie Berman
on the eve of
her marriage to
Sidney Stoller.

the armed forces. My father was a sharpshooter and sniper in places like Guadalcanal. After the war, Raymond went to medical school and Sidney went to work for my grandfather, which marked the birth of an enterprise called Stoller and Son, Inc., Carpentry Contractors. My father and grandfather's company helped to build suburban houses in Silver Spring, Maryland. Indeed, we lived in one of the houses my father and grandfather had built. Stoller and Son also did the carpentry work for many of the high-rise and garden apartments in the Washington, DC, metropolitan area.

My mother came from more modest circumstances. Her Jewish parents escaped from Latvia and made their way to Montreal, Canada. Eventually they moved from Montreal to Cambridge, Massachusetts. When his business prospects turned sour there, my maternal grandfather moved the family—two boys and three girls, including, of course, my mother, Goldie, to Washington, DC. On the streets of the nation's capital, my grandfather, Morris, became a fruit peddler. Unfortunately, he had a taste for gambling. He worked hard and earned money, which he squandered on pinochle and poker. Scrambling for income, my maternal grandmother, Leah, turned her home into a boardinghouse. My mother, then, grew up in a relatively poor Jewish home in which scant resources were reserved for the two boys in the household who, it was hoped, would eventually end the family's economic plight.

My parents met and fell in love during the hard times of the late 1930s. The uncertainties precipitated by the onslaught of World War II compelled them to postpone their wedding. When my father received his orders to ship out to the Pacific, my parents decided to get married. My mother went with my father to Brownsville, Texas, where he suffered through basic training. My father came back from World War II unscathed—physically at least. He never talked about what he had experienced in the sniper's perch or on the battlefield.

The business was very much a family-run enterprise. My uncle, who was, in fact, my father's sister's husband, did the books. My father's brother, Raymond, now a surgeon, provided some timely loans. There were many ups and downs in the construction business. Although Stoller and Son, Inc. was far from producing astronomical profits in the late 1950s, the business provided a good life for our family. Even so, it did not afford us a style of living that satisfied my parents.

Through talk at frequent family gatherings at the large home of my paternal grandparents, family members continuously cultivated in me a strong will to succeed, which for them meant the accumulation of wealth. They liked to tell me that you could find fortune through hard work or through marriage. My mother would always talk about young men from relatively modest means who married "rich girls," and lived "happily ever after." Everyone looked to my Uncle Ray, "The Doctor," as the great success story in the family. By the time I was ten years old, my uncle, who was my godfather, had moved back to the family digs in Detroit and had built a private medical clinic. It was said that Uncle Ray was a millionaire. In the eyes of the family, he had become the model of and for success.

Contrast my beginnings to those of Yaya. When Yaya was a young boy, he learned how to sell products at the Belayara market. In addition to going to the local elementary and secondary school, he spent the early evening hours memorizing the Koran under the guidance of a local cleric. Half a world away, my parents sent me to Hebrew School, where three after-school afternoons a week, I learned to read and write Hebrew—all in preparation for my bar mitzvah.

As I neared thirteen my parents planned a large celebration to fete the emergent "manhood" of their firstborn son. They invited hundreds of people, rented the auditorium of our synagogue, bought many cases of vodka, arranged for a catered sit-down dinner, and hired the Guy Davis orchestra, featuring Jose Vargas on maracas and vocals. They also sent me off to dance school, where the inestimable Groggy Gurwitz taught me how to fox-trot, cha-cha, polka, jitterbug, and rumba. For almost a year my mother dropped me off at Groggy's studio, where the slender, permanently tanned, peroxided and pompadoured dance instructor, who sometimes practiced law, showed us his moves. Even though I didn't particularly like my dance partners, twelve-year-old Jewish girls in training for their bat mitzvah, who, in retrospect, didn't care very much for me, Groggy's lessons gave me a ballroom dancing foundation. By February 6, 1960, I was ready to dance—and dance well—with my mother, grandmother,

and aunts—all part of the grand design to use my bar mitzvah
to *kvell* (beam with pride) about my family's relative prosperity.

During my childhood and adolescence some youth also received accolades from adults for "being smart," something
highly valued in urban Jewish culture of the 1950s and 1960s.[1]
This atmosphere compelled me to work very hard in high school.
I received fairly good grades and joined the debate team. If I
could get accepted to an Ivy League university, I'd feel like a success. Alas, my academic record put that dream pretty much out
of reach. What's more, no one in my family was a Harvard, Yale,
Columbia, or Penn alumnus, which meant that I had no chance
of being admitted as a "legacy" student. Several select liberal arts

colleges also rejected my application for admission. Finally, the University of Pittsburgh, which was a fine institution of higher learning, accepted me and off I went to college.

When my father drove me from Silver Spring to Pittsburgh the fear that pulsed through my body had little do to with leaving home for the first time. In fact, I had long looked forward to being more on my own. No, I feared the challenge of a higher education. Could I cut it? Would I prove wanting in the competition for grades at Pitt? Would they kick me out?

When I arrived on campus, unpacked, and wandered into what was for me a brave new world, I steeled my resolve to do well. Unlike my roommate and many of the students on my dorm floor, I spent much of my spare time studying. I thought that if I spent enough time reading and taking notes, the effort might make up for my self-perceived intellectual deficiencies.

I took my classes, studied like a fiend, and managed to make the dean's list my first semester. Perhaps I would be able to make my parents proud of me? Given my family history, I felt indirect pressure to pursue medicine and become a physician like my Uncle Ray. If that prestigious path didn't work out, I could always take courses that would prepare me for a legal career. My skills in science and math precluded the medical path, which meant that I decided to major in political science, a good course of study for a budding lawyer.

As I took more and more courses with some very well known political scientists, I quickly tired of the discipline. For reasons I still find unclear, I found literature and especially philosophy much more intriguing—especially the phenomenologically inspired philosophy of French thinkers like Jean-Paul Sartre and Maurice Merleau-Ponty. When I read Sartre, Camus, and Merleau-Ponty I imagined myself in Paris, seated at Les Deux Magots, talking philosophy. I found like-minded students in my dorm. We'd sit in the dorm café, drink coffee, smoke cigarettes, and discuss the whys and wherefores of Sartre's *Being and Noth-*

ingness or Merleau-Ponty's *The Phenomenology of Perception*. Sometimes our spirited discussions would linger into the wee hours of the morning.[2]

My interest in reading and discussing philosophy eventually drew me toward writing. In my youthful imagination, I thought it would be wonderful to live the writing life. I wondered if I could transform the deep wisdom of continental philosophy into highly engaging stories. In short, I wanted to be a novelist.

None of my professors directly encouraged me to pursue the writing life.

"It's a tough path," they said.

"You'd be better off doing something else."

Some of them recommended that I try journalism. If I liked writing for newspapers or magazines, they suggested, I might want to extend my writing to short stories and novels. Following their advice, I began to write for the student newspaper, the *Pitt News*, first as a reporter, then as news editor, and finally, in my senior year, as editor in chief.

That year, 1968–69, turned out to be one of the most momentous periods in American history—the assassinations of Martin Luther King and Bobby Kennedy, Lyndon Johnson's refusal to run for a second term, the escalation of the war in Vietnam, and the exponential growth of the antiwar movement on college campuses. We covered all of it and I wrote many editorials against the war in Vietnam as well as diatribes that condemned the FBI's antidemocratic practices.

Amid the social and political chaos of 1968–69, my parents wondered about my future. Did I still plan on going to law school? What would I do to earn a living? Where did I want to live after graduation? What did I want to do about the draft?

During my junior year of college, I read philosophy, wrote newspaper articles, and remained silent about my future plans. Toward the beginning of my senior year, though, my mother pressed the issue.

FIGURE 13. Paul Stoller at the *Pitt News*, 1968–69.

"What are you going to do, Paul?" she asked during one of our routine phone conversations.

The gig was up. "I want to be a writer," I confessed.

"But there's no money in that, Paul."

"That doesn't matter to me," I said.

"Well, it matters to us. How will you support a family as a writer?"

"Things will work out."

"We thought you wanted to be a lawyer," she stated.

"That's what you wanted for me," I stated. "I don't want to be a lawyer."

"Can you do just one thing for me?"

"Sure, Mom."

"Just take the law school test and apply to one law school. Can you do that?"

Because she seemed so troubled, I agreed to her request. Following our conversation, I took the LSAT and received a fair to middling score. Honoring my commitment, I applied to one law school—Harvard. In what seemed record time, the admissions committee at Harvard Law School rejected my application.

Meanwhile, the war in Vietnam continued to escalate. Some of my classmates had been drafted and had gone to Vietnam. Several of them had been killed in action. The location of my draft board in suburban Silver Spring, an area with a significant population of draft-age college students, meant that many of my fellow residents could be drafted at any time. My mother, who then worked for the District of Columbia city government, had National Guard connections. If I agreed, she could arrange for me to become a National Guardsman, which would have decreased the likelihood of my being sent to Vietnam.

"I don't want to be in the National Guard," I told her, appreciating deeply her efforts on my behalf. "I've been accepted for graduate study at the Northwestern University's Medill School of Journalism. It's one of the best in the country," I told her.

"That's terrific," she retorted, "but they will draft you anyway."

"I'll figure out something."

She was worried and unconvinced.

Not long thereafter, I wandered over to a rundown basement office near campus to see a Peace Corps recruiter. Fred was short and thin and had long brown unkempt hair, a scraggly beard. He loved the Peace Corps. He told me that because I had studied French, I would be a prime candidate for a Francophone Africa assignment. What's more, Peace Corps service would provide me an occupational deferment from the draft. Peace Corps, he explained, would give me additional language training in French and might, depending upon the West African country I selected, instruct me in an African language. In exchange, I would have to put my graduate education in journalism on hold for two years and exist on a meager living allowance. "You won't be saving much money in Peace Corps," he said.

I applied and several months later was accepted as a Peace Corps volunteer for Francophone West Africa, where volunteers then worked in Senegal, Upper Volta (now Burkina Faso), Côte d'Ivoire, Togo, Dahomey (now Benin), Niger, and Chad. After I graduated from Pitt in May 1969, I returned home to Silver Spring for one month. My parents reluctantly accepted the independence of my thought and wished me well. In June I traveled to Philadelphia to begin my Peace Corps experience. I joined more than two hundred other volunteers who were also headed to West Africa.

On our first night in Philadelphia, C. Payne Lucas, who in 1969 was Africa regional director for the Peace Corps, spoke to us about Africa. He said that in exchange for our service, we could expect to reap rich rewards. Lucas had been the Peace Corps director in Niger, and he spoke movingly about one of the poorest places in the world.

"Niger doesn't have a lot of money or much in the way of natural resources," he said. "It does have a whole lot of sand," he stated. "The people there are terribly poor, but instead of complaining, they are full of life. After you spend some time in Niger, all that sand begins to look like gold."

At that moment I knew I wanted to spend my two-year stint in Niger.

So we headed off to La Pocatière, Quebec, a town on the southern bank of the Saint Lawrence River, some eighty miles northeast of Quebec City, for six weeks of immersion training in French. Peace Corps then shipped us off to Côte d'Ivoire by way of Paris and Monrovia.

I will never forget my first moments in Africa. We had taken a night flight from Paris–Le Bourget to Monrovia, where we landed just after dawn in a steamy fog.

"You need to stay on the aircraft," we were told. "We'll be here for about one hour, but breakfast will be brought on board."

The flight attendants opened the doors, which allowed fetid air—African air—to stream into the plane. After an uncomfortable night, the volunteers grumbled about the conditions. I began to sweat profusely.

"How long will we have to wait in this inferno?" I asked Mike, my seatmate, whom I found cool and collected.

"Shouldn't be too long," he said rather cheerfully. "We finally made it to Africa," he said, slapping me on my shoulder.

At that moment the young, draft-dodging Jewish boy from Silver Spring, Maryland, was considerably less cheerful. Had I made the right decision?

After what seemed an interminable amount of time, women dressed in crisply starched white uniforms—skirts and short-sleeved white blouses with epaulettes, no less, brought each of us a box with a cup of yogurt, a banana, a croissant, and a wedge of butter. They also served us a cup of tea and provided sugar cubes and a small carton of milk. Starved, I plunged into my breakfast, consuming my banana and yogurt in a less than a minute. Wanting to savor what I considered a delicacy, I approached the croissant with great anticipation. I took a bite and discovered that a green bug had been baked into it.

Observing my horror, cool and collected Mike slapped me on the shoulder. "Welcome to Africa, Paul."[3]

5 ::: STUMBLING INTO ANTHROPOLOGY IN NIGER

After the stop in Monrovia, we flew to Abidjan, which I soon left and headed north to Niger, where I continued to learn French and began to learn the Songhay language. My Songhay teachers would send my fellow students and me to the market with lists of items to buy, compelling us to communicate with people in Songhay. When we returned to the classroom, they would ask us to draw a market map and label its components—also in Songhay. Those were confusing times for a twenty-two-year-old pacifist who hadn't wanted to fight a war he didn't believe in. After one month of intensive Songhay, I took the bus—a local rather than express—for Tera, the Songhay town in which I would teach English as a Foreign Language to secondary-school students. Due to frequent tire changes, a problematic Niger River ferry, prayer breaks, police inspections, and the driver's visit to a riverside market, the 180-kilometer trip took twelve hot hours to complete.

I joined a faculty of three French "cooperants" who, in lieu of compulsory military service, volunteered their pedagogical talents for two years in Tera, Niger. The principal, a rather disagreeable and racist Frenchman, and a Nigerien science teacher completed our teaching team. The campus consisted of three dormitories, five faculty houses, a refectory, and a faculty kitchen. There was a water tower and a generator for local power. Unfortunately, nothing worked at the school. The generator had broken the year before, which meant that the water tower didn't function, let alone the ceiling fans in our faculty bungalows. Because there was no money to fix school equipment, the school arranged for students to live with families in town. Our faculty kitchen had a large temperamental kerosene refrigerator. When it worked we had ice and fresh food. When it didn't work we had to throw away our food. During the heat of day, we took our meals inside our faculty dining room, which was next to the kitchen. At night, we set up a large table on the sandy school grounds and lit a Petromax lamp, the bright light of which attracted every imaginable insect in the neighborhood. By that time, the bugs did not bother me. They routinely landed in my evening soup. When that happened I followed the lead of my colleagues: find the critter with my spoon, scoop it up, throw it onto the sand, and continue eating.

As I mentioned, I taught English as a Foreign Language. Upon learning that I played the guitar, the principal made me the music teacher. Hearing about my love of exercise he also designated me the physical education teacher. Although I confessed to knowing little about soccer, he insisted that I be the soccer coach.

In a setting where nothing worked, we adjusted to the environment. Despite an admittedly surprising capacity to adapt to these conditions, I couldn't accept the French principal's racist behavior. He cursed at the Africans in our midst, often comparing them to ignorant, less-than-human beasts. In response, our Songhay cooks and custodians used Songhay to make disparaging remarks about him. When at dinner, the principal insulted our cook, Yacouba, the latter said: "Ni nga ngoko," a Songhay epithet that means "Fuck your mother." When the principal asked me what Yacouba had said, I professed my ignorance. "My Songhay is not that advanced," I said.

The principal's racist behavior created a lot of tension at the secondary school, which meant that when my colleagues invited me for beer, I happily agreed to go to Chez Jacob, the only bar in town. Situated in Zongo, the neighborhood for non-Songhay immigrants to Tera, Chez Jacob, owned by a Yoruba from Nigeria, consisted of a relatively small rectangular mud-brick structure that featured a well-stocked kerosene refrigerator and two benches, which, by the time we arrived in late afternoon, had been placed in a small courtyard just beyond the establishment's front door.

We used these occasions to drink one-liter bottles of Kronenbourg beer, discuss the trials and tribulations of our students, the scope of politics in Niger, and not least, the racist attitudes and behavior of our school principal. Toward the end of the school year at one of our late afternoon sessions, the sounds and sights of a spirit possession ceremony unfolded in their full glory right next to us.

Unbeknownst to us, the local spirit possession priest lived next door to Chez Jacob. I had never seen anything like a spirit possession ceremony: the whine of the melodic one-string violin, the clack of gourd drums, dancers kicking up dust as they twirled about the sandy dance grounds. Among the dancers there appeared a man dressed in a white laboratory coat who bellowed like an animal. An elder from the town insisted that I meet this man who appeared to be talking in Pidgin French. As saliva frothed from his mouth and his eyes blazed, this terrifying figure extended his hand to me. When I shook his hand, our contact provoked physical as well as psychological shock. I had had my first contact with a Hauka, a Songhay spirit that mimics figures from the colonial past.

At that moment I stepped over the line that had separated my being from that of someone like Yaya. That one step changed my life immeasurably.[1]

My electro-contact with *lokotoro*, the Hauka spirit known as "The Doctor," not only shook the foundations of my carefully crafted world but also bolstered my inner resolve. I confronted the racist school principal and told him that I found his ideas and behavior despicable—beneath contempt. "I will not return here next year," I informed him. "I cannot work with a racist."

He remained silent.

"I've already put in for a transfer," I told him, "and have been informed that you'll get another Peace Corps volunteer next year."

He smirked. "I'll not stand in your way. You won't be missed."

: : :

My transfer went through and I spent my second Peace Corps year in Tillabéri, Niger, a larger town than Tera. The town hugged the east bank of the Niger River some 120 kilometers north of Niger's capital, Niamey. In Tillabéri, the school equipment worked. We usually had electricity for several hours each day. My bungalow was dusty, but spacious. The proximity of the Niger River translated into an abundance of water, which meant the barrel that supplied water for showers and toilet necessities was always filled. In Tillabéri the principal was a short, thin Nigerien math professor named Amadu Adamu. The faculty consisted of a group of cheery Frenchmen along with a several Nigerien educators. The Nigeriens taught geography and physical education.

I settled into a rather enjoyable routine. I taught in the mornings and afternoons and consumed sumptuous lunches and dinners with my French friends. In the late afternoon, I would take out a dugout on the glorious Niger River or ride a powerful Arabian stallion into the desert scrub, sometimes galloping up to the summit of a particular butte that, at dusk, provided an awe-inspiring view of the majestic Niger River valley. Sometimes I would forego a late afternoon ride to pop over to the Giraffe Bar to drink beer with fellow Americans—a crazy crew of characters: a drugged hippie type; a model "on break" from the exigencies of the fashion world; a few very serious save-the-world activists; and my favorite person, Dale, a tall and bone thin and mustachioed man who hailed from eastern Kentucky. The Peace Corps had trained him to organize villagers to dig new wells, which in the bush would ensure a cleaner and more regular source of water. My friend looked like the actor Dennis Weaver who played Chester on the 1950s television series *Gunsmoke*.

For six months or so I lived a kind of bohemian dream that I could never have imagined in the comfortable and protective surroundings of my childhood and adolescence. Outside my comfort zone in Tillabéri, I wrote every day, both prose and poetry, and made daily entries in a journal—stuff I wanted to one day transform into a polished work of fiction.

Sometimes, though, an alternate reality would unexpectedly burst the bubble of my illusory dreams. One morning in one of my English classes, I noticed a female student, Zeinabou, scratching herself as she fidgeted in her seat. She was among the most attractive of my students: tall, slender, with an oval face featuring high cheekbones offset by large dark brown eyes. Her looks brought her much attention—some wanted, some not so desired—from fellow students and from local civil servants. On that morning her uncomfortable state didn't immediately precipitate concern. She might not have slept well. She might be hungry or ill. What's more, no one else in the class had seemed to notice her discomfort.

Deep moans suddenly transformed calm into chaos—at least for me. Zeinabou had stood up. Her eyes burned. She pulled out large tufts of her hair. She spoke in Pidgin French. I first thought she had had a mental breakdown, but the students laughed at her.

"What's going on?" I asked.

"It's her spirit," one of the students said, rather nonchalantly. "We should take her to the principal's office."

We slowly took her, twitching and screaming, to Amadu Adamu's office. The principal looked at his student and sighed.

"First one this year," he said. "The spirits like to take the bodies of our young people. Looks like a Hauka has gotten a hold of Zeinabou."

"Will she be okay?" I asked.

Amadu Adamu shrugged. "She just needs to get initiated. Once that happens she'll be fine." He chuckled. "Haven't you seen possession, Monsieur Paul?"

"Once, but not in my classroom."

The principal hunched his shoulders. "It happens around here."

The Hauka had suddenly returned to my life—in my classroom! This event unsettled me. I needed explanations and guidance, but my French and Nigerien colleagues advised me to move on. They said that spirit possession was no big deal; it occurred regularly in Tillabéri—even in classrooms. They said that it could be emotionally dangerous for me to dwell on the local spirits.

I tried to put what I had seen out of my mind, but the image of Zeinabou screaming as she pulled out her hair remained imprinted in my consciousness. Granted, I was still able to teach, take canoe trips, go horseback riding, and drink beer with my buddies at the Giraffe Bar, but I had detected an existential shift in my being. I wanted to learn more about these spirits and spirit possession ceremonies.

In the afternoons I worked on my journal and a novel. Searing heat and intermittent electricity slowed the pace of these thought-filled but uneventful afternoons. Late one afternoon, though, I tuned in to the drum rhythms coming from atop the sand dune that rose up like a mound beyond my bungalow. I had heard these echoing sounds before but hadn't taken much notice of them. That afternoon I decided to investigate. I left my bungalow and trudged up the dune toward a compound of straw huts bordered by a low fence fashioned from dried millet stalks. As I got closer I heard the high-pitched sound. It sounded like the violin I had heard in Tera. I walked into the area to see a crowd of people gathered around a thatched canopy under which three drummers struck gourds buried in the sand. Behind the drummers a violinist played his one stringed instrument with gusto. Men and women formed a line. One by one they moved toward the musicians. They stomped on the sand and flapped their arms in sync with the music.

This ceremony seemed similar to the one I had seen in Tera but appeared to be more organized. A short frail old man dressed in black robes and a black turban brought me a flimsy folding chair and asked me to sit down.

"I'm Adamu Jenitongo," he said, smiling. His black eyes burned with intensity. "This is my house. Welcome to our ceremony."

"What do you call it?"

"It's a party for the spirits," he said. "If you wait long enough, a spirit may ride the body of one of the dancers."

Other people came over to greet me.

"Welcome to our group," one person said.

"Do you like our music?" another person asked.

"Can you dance?" a man asked me.

"No."

"I'll show you."

With that he took my hand and led me to the dance grounds. Seeing me, the musicians picked up the tempo. Using every skill I had learned from the irrepressible Groggy Gurwitz, I followed the man's lead and moved my body to the rhythm. The audience applauded the clumsy, but well-intentioned efforts of a neophyte.

Soon after I sat down and caught my breath, a tall and fleshly woman strolled onto the dance grounds. Suddenly her body shook violently. Tears streamed from her eyes. She began to sing in a high-pitched squeaky voice. She tore off her top and scooped up sand and showered it on her body.

The old man, Adamu Jenitongo, stood next to me. "We are blessed today. A Black Spirit has visited us. It is washing with the sand, and that is good for our town."

Completely dumbfounded, I remained silent.

"You have brought us good fortune," Adamu Jenitongo stated. He asked my name.

By that time, the sun had begun to set.

"Paul," Adamu Jenitongo said, "You danced. That shows your respect for us and for the spirits. You must come again. When you hear the music, come and visit us."

I spent many afternoons in Adamu Jenitongo's compound. Usually I went there to witness a spirit possession ceremony. Sometimes, I'd simply go there to talk with the old man. Toward the end of my Peace Corps service, I told Adamu Jenitongo that I would soon be returning to the United States.

At our last meeting, he held my hand and thanked me for my visits. He smiled at me and said, "You'll be back."

: : :

When I was stepping gingerly through the portal of Songhay spirit possession, Yaya had already plunged into the world of long-distance trade. He had left Belayara and had settled with his older brother in Abidjan. As in my case, his world would never be the same.

At the time, I hadn't known that Adamu Jenitongo was not only a *zima*, a spirit possession priest, but was also the most powerful sorcerer in all of western Niger, a man who could see the past, know the present, and divine the future. What I did know, though, was that I wanted to find a way to get back to Niger, to Tillabéri and the Songhay world of spirits. I enrolled in graduate school, first in linguistics and then, after earning a master of science degree, in social anthropology. The excitement of first debating the complex rules of Noam Chomsky's transformational linguistics and then the thrill of pondering the multiple oppositions of Claude Lévi-Strauss's elegant form of structuralism led me away from the gritty challenge of confronting the reality of spirit possession in Adamu Jenitongo's Tillabéri compound. In graduate school, I read deeply and widely—extending my appreciation for Chomsky and Lévi-Strauss, but also for continental philosophers like Jean-Paul Sartre, Maurice Merleau-

Ponty, and later, Jacques Derrida and Roland Barthes. Returning to my earlier interests in existentialism and phenomenology, my orientation to anthropology took on philosophical dimensions. For my dissertation I proposed an ethnography of communication that would consider religious discourse in a local Nigerien setting. I wanted to consider the existential contours of religious language in Islamic (the Friday mosque) and in non-Islamic (spirit possession ceremonies) contexts.

With the guidance of my mentors at the University of Texas at Austin, I received funding for a project that would take me back to Niger for one year of field research. I planned to spend the year in Mehanna, a large market town on the west bank of the Niger River some 180 kilometers north of Niger's capital, Niamey. And so I got my shots, bought a camera, a tape recorder, and supplied myself with audio tapes, film—both black-and-white and color—a good pair of walking boots, a water filter, and a portable Smith Corona typewriter. After a few months of patient waiting, I received my research authorization from the government of Niger, signed by General Seyni Kountche, then president of the republic.

When I arrived in Niamey, I took up residence in a small monk-like room at the Social Sciences Research Institute. There I met Nigerien colleagues and arranged for my credentials to be sent to the local administrators who governed the regions where I planned to conduct research. While I waited for my colleagues to make these arrangements, I spent time in the library reading hard-to-find historical texts on local societies.

One morning I noticed a white man sitting alone on a ledge at the edge the institute grounds. He wore khakis and a light blue shirt. His blue socks matched the color of his shirt. A blue ascot had been expertly tied around his neck. The man, who had a round face, little hair, and large penetrating blue eyes, smiled at me with warmth.

"Hello," he said. "Can I help you?"

Who was this out-of-place guy, I wondered. "I'm a researcher here," I said. "I'm waiting for final authorization to go to the bush."

"Are you an anthropologist?" he asked.

"I am," I answered.

"Where are you headed?"

"Mehanna."

He slapped his hand on his thigh. "I know Mehanna," he said. "I spent time there."

"You did?"

"Several years ago."

My curiosity finally got the best of me. "My name is Paul Stoller," I stated. "Can I ask your name, Monsieur?"

"Of course," he said smiling radiantly. "I'm Jean Rouch."

"Oh my God!" I exclaimed. "Please excuse my impertinence Monsieur Rouch. I've read all your books and I've seen many of your films. I hope I haven't insulted you."

"Not at all my friend," he responded. "From now on, just call me Jean."

"Okay," I said a bit flabbergasted.

He asked me to sit next to him. We talked at length about Songhay religion, history, and society.

By the time the lunch hour arrived, Jean Rouch stood up, dusted off his trousers, and extended his hand to me. "I enjoyed our conversation very much. I'd rather talk with you than meet an annoying minister for lunch." He shrugged, and then winked at me. "Paul," he said channeling Humphrey Bogart in *Casablanca*, "I think this is the beginning of a beautiful friendship."

: : :

Jean Rouch's endorsement filled me with energy and excitement. In short order I received final research authorization and headed out to my field site—Mehanna. Before I set foot in Mehanna, though, I needed to check in with the regional administrator, a slender, intense, and rather officious man. When we met in his dusty office he wondered why in hell's name someone like me wanted to spend time in the bush.

"There's no clean water in Mehanna," he warned me. "And if you need a doctor, you'll have to come back here to Tera. The roads are bad and there are hardly any trucks that could evacuate you."

"That's okay," I said with no small amount of insouciance. "I'm young and healthy."

The administrator rolled his eyes. "You'll need a horse or camel to get around," he advised.

"That's what I thought."

"I've got a big truck going there tomorrow morning. You can get a ride on it. My friend, Boureima Boulhassane, is headed down there. He's from Mehanna and he'll tell you what to expect."

The next morning I got on a Mehanna-bound Berliet, a massive truck used to negotiate the sandy tracks that traverse the Sahara. A mountainous pile of surplus grain had been loaded into the bay. In the three-seat cabin, I found myself squeezed between a silent driver and Boureima, who proudly informed me in impeccable French that he was from a family of Songhay nobles.

"I can trace my roots all the way back to Askia Mohammed Toure, the great king of the sixteenth-century Songhay Empire."

After that rather immodest admission, we lapsed into silence. As the sun rose higher in the sky and a haze settled into the air, we chugged up sand dunes and skirted across plains of pebble-strewn scrub brush dotted with occasional water holes. Looking ahead, I would occasionally steal a glance at Boureima, who sat there giving me an irascible stare.

"You know," he said, finally breaking our uncomfortable silence, "you Europeans can't possibly live in a desolate place like Mehanna. I can't even spend more than a day or two there."

As we rolled through Kokoro, a village situated along a very long and large waterhole, he realized that his advice had fallen on deaf ears.

"I can see you're stubborn," he said with a deep frown and furrowed brow. Boureima was slight, rather short, and palpably intense.

"I am."

"Well, then, you can stay in my family compound. It's right in the center of town, next to the market and stone's throw from the riverbank."

"Sounds perfect."

"The compound comes with Sidi, the caretaker. He'll make sure you have water and wood. He'll arrange for someone to cook your meals. All you need to do is pay me $40. That will take care of the rent for several months. Don't pay Sidi more than $20 a month."

As we sealed these arrangements, the truck crested a very steep dune. In the distance we saw the glistening waters of the Niger River. A green cluster of trees marked Mehanna's village space.

"That's your new home," Boureima said.

"How long will you stay?" I asked.

"I'll go to today's market, spend the night and leave in the morning. A dugout will take me to the Bonfebba market on the east bank of the river. From there I catch a bush taxi to Niamey."

When I arrived at Mehanna I stumbled upon a huge multi-ethnic market. I saw indigo veiled Tuareg men atop camels bearing loads of Saharan rock salt. Tuareg smiths offered knives holstered in colorful dyed leather and tasseled sheaves. The smiths also displayed similarly tooled horse and camel saddles, leather satchels, and long leather pillows. Seated on palm frond mats, Fulan women sold sour milk and butter; and Hausa butchers sold raw, fly-covered beef and mutton as well as roasted brochettes and a spicy jerky, called *kilishi*. Songhay women presented spices and cloth. Yoruba from Nigeria hawked nails, screws, tin, and other items of hardware.

When I climbed down from the truck's cabin, a crowd of people gathered. Staring at me with open-mouthed dumbfound expressions, they bantered in Songhay, wondering what the white man was doing in Mehanna.

Boureima waved them off. "Haven't you ever seen a white man before?" he chided them in Songhay. "Go away."

"I may be a white man," I said to them in Songhay, "but I do speak some Songhay."

They gasped and peppered me with scores of questions. How did I learn Songhay? How long would I stay? What was I going to do?

Boureima steered me to edge of the market and introduced me to Mehanna's chief, who greeted me warmly and invited me to lunch in his compound.

During our lunch I explained my project. He seemed uninterested. He wanted to know where the white man would live. "The last white man who lived here had a small house on the outskirts of town. You could live there," he suggested.

"Well . . ."

"That's where Monsieur Rouch lived."

"When did he live there?"

"I was very young. Maybe thirty years ago."

Boureima interjected. "He's going to live in our compound. It's better if he lives in the center of town."

"But Monsieur Rouch . . ."

Boureima interrupted the chief. "It's all arranged. He's paid rent."

After lunch, Boureima and the chief escorted me to the new house and introduced me to Sidi, the caretaker.

I spent one year in Mehanna. After an initial two months of very hard work on a census I learned that if you asked questions in the wrong way, people would lie to you. In response to my rather ethnocentrically constructed questionnaire on family structure, linguistic competence, and ethnic identity every one of the 180 respondents had, in fact, lied. Taking pity on the hapless young European, the village elders told me to stop asking questions.

"If you want to learn about us," one man said, "you must open your ears and listen to the elders."

I followed their advice and learned a great deal about social life in Mehanna. Six months into my fieldwork about the use of ritual language in Islam and in spirit possession ceremonies, I felt good about my progress and wondered what Jean Rouch would think about a study being conducted in village where he had once spent time. I took a wide range of photographs, tape-recorded interviews with elders, and recorded spirit possession music. I also captured on tape the wide-ranging stylized talk of spirits speaking through the bodies of their mediums. One afternoon while I typed field notes in my house a bird shat on my head. Djibo, a rice farmer who witnessed this travesty, jumped up for joy.

"I've seen something," he said.

"No shit," I retorted.

"No, it's a sign. I am a *sorko* (a kind of Songhay healer) and you have been pointed out to me. You must come to my compound tonight to begin to learn about sorcery."[2]

So began a seventeen-year sojourn along the byways of Songhay sorcery and witchcraft.[3] After weeks of memorizing incantations and learning about herbal as well as magical medicines, Djibo and his father, Mounmouni, prepared me a batch of *kusu*, or magic cake. Mounmouni put water in a small pot, also called *kusu* in Songhay, and spread plant powder in concentric circles along the water's surface. He then recited a number of incantations, including the *genji how*, literally, tying up the bush, which seeks to control the dangerous forces of uncontrolled (bush as opposed to village) space. When he completed the incantations, he spat into the mixture so that, as he put it, the words of the ancestors would mix with the substances.

Mounmouni smiled at me. "This is food with no sauce. It gives you force. You'll need it now."

"It's not easy to eat, but you must finish all of it," Djibo said.

They left me to eat alone in the dim light of Djibo's two-room mud-brick house. As I stared at the small bowl of kusu, my mind filled with thoughts. What was this young Jewish boy from Silver Spring, Maryland, doing in that dim and dank room halfway around the world? If I ate this weird stuff, would I suddenly become different? Would my world be changed forever? What would Jean Rouch do?

With great trepidation, I ate the paste, which immediately bloated me and made me feel slightly nauseous. My initiators soon returned to compliment me on having eaten all of the kusu. Djibo informed me that the kusu had connected my body to the spirit world. I couldn't imagine how that could be possible.

Thereafter, Mounmouni and Djibo insisted that I watch them practice the healing arts. When sick people came to visit their compound, I got to observe firsthand how they mixed medicines and how they recited incantations. On some occasions I went with Djibo to treat clients, which gave me a window into his world. It quickly became apparent that he had the capacity to heal people suffering from physical ailments and psychological disorders. Even if the strong force of witchcraft had made them seriously ill, most of Djibo's patients seemed to recover.

My initiator liked to talk about his special capacities. He told me of his travel to a special village, the home of powerful spirits that dwell "under" the Niger River. To prove his point he gave me some soil from that underwater village.

"It's soil that will not get wet," he said.

He shaped a small hill of it on a stone and then immersed it in a bowl of water. The soil took on a metallic sheen, but kept its shape. When he raised the soil from the water, it was bone dry.

"That," he said, "is the magic of the sorko."[4]

:::

Toward the end of that first year of fieldwork, Djibo and his father summoned me to the latter's compound of straw huts, which was on a dune that formed the southern edge of Mehanna. The men welcomed me into the cool shade of the hut and asked me to sit down on a palm frond mat.

"Are there new incantations to learn?" I asked. "Do you have new medicines to show me?"

Mounmouni Kada spit out some chewing tobacco. With his piercing eyes, he peered into my being. Then he smiled and spat again. "Not today, my son," he said. "We could teach you much more, but our work is finished."

"But I would like to learn more."

"You will," the old man said, "but not from us. We are sending you to sit with our teacher in Tillabéri. He'll take up the burden of your learning."

"Who is this man?" I asked.

"You know him," Djibo said. "He's the old spirit priest in Tillabéri who lives behind the school."

"Adamu Jenitongo?" I asked.

"You know him as a spirit priest, but he's also a great healer in our part of Niger," Djibo continued. "He's our master and he's summoned you to sit with him—a great honor."

I'll be damned.

That year the arrival of the Nigerien hot season coincided with my departure from Mehanna. In searing heat, I packed my gear, said my good-byes, and loaded my stuff into a leaky dugout canoe. We shoved off going south and east toward the market town of Bonfebba. There I hauled my gear to a beat-up Toyota minivan headed toward Niamey. Assistants tied my bags to the taxi's roof and we chugged off toward Tillabéri, a short forty kilometers to the south. Because we didn't have a flat tire, engine trouble, and didn't run out of gas, we made it to the Tillabéri depot in record time—about two hours.

At midday several depot workers off-loaded my belongings. I grabbed my gear and walked toward the secondary school where I had once taught and then headed up to the summit of a familiar dune. I clapped three times outside the entrance of the very compound where I had, years before, witnessed spirit possession ceremonies. On seeing me, children announced the arrival of a white man. Soon thereafter, Adamu Jenitongo, dressed in faded and frayed black robes and his ever-present black turban, walked toward me with a broad smile on his face. He extended his hand and I shook it.

"Welcome, Paul. What took you so long?"

: : :

From that moment in May 1976, I began to "sit" with Adamu Jenitongo. During our first session, my mentor set the moral compass of our relationship.

"If you want to learn about healing and power," he said, "you and I have to create a relationship of trust. If your character is clean, our trust will grow strong. If your character is dirty, our trust will be betrayed and our relationship will be broken. In time, I will know the depth of your character which will tell me if we should move forward together."

Speechless, I shook my head.

"In everything you do," he said pointing his finger at me, "remember this: 'Say what you mean and do what you say.'" "If you do that," he continued, "people will know who you are and will trust you to heal them."

At first, I stayed with colleagues at the secondary school and would visit my teacher in what he called "the black of night," a time when you could talk about powerful words and plants in relative privacy. I would march up the dune at midnight and quietly make my way to Adamu Jenitongo's straw hut, the spirit hut. That's where he stored all of his sacred objects: a hatchet with a bell associated with Dongo, spirit of thunder; small leather sandals for the *Atakurma*, the elves of the Songhay bush; a tall iron staff—the *lolo* of *sohanci* sorcerers—on which you found copper and brass rings encrusted with years of sacrificial blood. In the dull flicker of a kerosene lantern, Adamu Jenitongo taught me incantations and described the healing properties of hundreds of medicinal plants. He showed me his divination shells—single-valve cowries—as well as the intricacies of geomancy.

At first I wanted to learn everything I could—and quickly.

Adamu Jenitongo laughed at my youthful exuberance. "It takes many, many years to learn *korte* [or magic]." Toward the end of June 1977, he announced that our sessions had come to an end. "You have to come back and live here with me in the spirit hut. Then we'll continue."

That statement set the pattern for my education in things Songhay. I spent as much time as I could in Niger, managing to travel to Tillabéri, Niger, during breaks from teaching. Upon my return each year, Adamu Jenitongo would greet me and teach me something new about the sorcerer's path.

During those times, Adamu Jenitongo also sent me to sit with practitioners from Wanzerbe, the famous village of sorcerers perched among the desiccated steppes and majestic dunes of northwestern Niger. There I eventually met Kassey, a diminutive grandmother, who was perhaps the most powerful of all sorcerers in Niger. In Wanzerbe I suffered two bouts of "sickness"—a temporary paralysis in the legs and presence of a small egg in my stool, the sign of impending death by sorcery. Adamu Jenitongo said the jealousy of his rivals had triggered the events, one of which occurred in 1979 and the other in 1984.[5]

After the first event, he complimented me on surviving. "You are well on the path," he told me.

After the second event, I told him that I couldn't go on.

"Don't worry about that attack, Paul," he said. "You are still here and now know that the path of power is very dangerous."

"Yes, indeed, Baba, but I don't want to follow it, anymore."

Adamu Jenitongo chuckled. "Well, then, you'll have to learn about medicine on the path of plants."

From then on we'd sit together in the "black of night" and discuss the properties of medicinal plants. Adamu Jenitongo demonstrated a remarkable knowledge of the local flora and how they could be used to treat a wide variety of disorders—malaria, asthma, skin infections, intestinal parasites, and hepatitis. He knew that if you picked a plant during daylight, its leaves or stems would have one kind of bodily impact, and that if you picked the same plant at night, its leaves or stems would have a different curative effect. He knew that for some plants, you could only use the root to heal people. He also taught me that certain resins could be burned to produce sedative effects in cases of extreme anxiety. During the same time period, he showed me how to sharpen my skills in divination, which had been and still are admittedly weak.

In the summer of 1987 I spent several months with my mentor. During previous visits Adamu Jenitongo's vigor had always surprised me. He walked miles every day and attended to his spiritual duties with an awe-inspiring robustness. In 1987, though, I found him a shadow of his former self. He didn't venture away from his dune-top compound, and his increasing fatigue prompted him to take long siestas and retire early in the evening. His oldest son, Moussa, explained that his father had been suffering from prostate cancer and that he would probably die in the coming months.

Despite these considerable difficulties, Adamu Jenitongo continued to heal people. He also organized several spirit possession ceremonies in his compound. Our lessons on the path of plants continued, though we had to schedule them early in the evening. By the time the "black of night" arrived, Adamu Jenitongo had long been in a sound sleep.

There were no special words that we exchanged the last time I saw my mentor. We talked about plants and the state of the world that the forces of change had inexorably altered. One last time, I asked him why he had taught me, a white man, so much about his world.

"It's because I like you," he said, giving me the same answer that he always gave to that question.

I left Niger several days later. A month after I returned home, I received word that the physical condition of my mentor had deteriorated. He had been to Niamey where he had undergone prostate surgery. By the time he returned home, his weak physical condition confined him to bed. As word spread about his condition, visitors began to come to Tillabéri, sometimes from great distances, to pay him their respects. Although weak in body, Adamu Jenitongo's mind and spirit remained strong. He regaled the well-wishers with a wide variety of stories from his long and well-lived life.

From then on I received regular updates about my mentor's health. In early March 1988, however, I received a phone call that he was gravely ill. I made rapid plans to fly to Niger. Two days later I arrived in Tillabéri only to learn that Adamu Jenitongo had died the day before. His oldest son took me to my mentor's final resting place, where I spoke heartfelt words into a stone and placed it on his grave.

Coming upon the grave, I wondered how I would go on. I had intellectual reasons for continuing my work in Niger, but I then came to the full realization that it had been love for Adamu Jenitongo that had inspired my dogged pursuit of Songhay sorcery and healing. What now? I wondered.

On our walk back to the dune-top compound, Moussa said something that shifted my attention. "Have you ever wondered," he asked me, "why Baba wanted to teach you so many of our secrets?"

"I asked him many times, but he just said that he liked me."

"He loved you like a son, Paul. But that's not the reason."

"I didn't think so."

"He took you on because my brother and I weren't ready to learn the powerful and important things he wanted to teach us. So he taught many things to you, knowing that after he was gone, you'd teach them to us. He made you the link between him and us."

It made perfect sense. "And now what?"

"You must meet your obligations to him and to us."

"I will."

When we got back to the dune-top compound, Moussa gave me rings and medicines that his father had left to me. Following again his father's instructions, he also divided up Adamu Jenitongo's objects. His brother received objects associated with spirit possession. Moussa took objects and medicines used in sorcery and healing. After spending several days with the family, I left for the United States. I returned to Tillabéri in December 1988 to attend Adamu Jenitongo's *kuma*, a ceremony that marks the end of mourning the death of a spirit possession priest.

For that ceremony, which was held on a Thursday, the day of the spirits, all the people that Adamu Jenitongo had helped (spirit mediums, people he had healed, and apprentices, a group that totaled more than 150) assembled at the dune-top compound and marched into the bush. We stopped at a fork in the path under a tamarind tree. There, the spirit priest from the next town, Tillakaina, officiated. He spoke movingly of my mentor. He then recited a text over a large pot in which he had mixed perfumes and plants. He poured the ablution into smaller pots and asked those who had been closest to Adamu Jenitongo, including me, to come up, take a pot, go into the bush, and wash the filth of death from our bodies.

That done, we returned to the compound, where the neighboring priest staged a possession ceremony during which spirits mounted the bodies of their mediums to pay homage to a great man. This ceremony lasted until sunset.

I spent the next several days talking about plants to my mentor's sons. They asked questions, which I tried to answer. They wanted demonstrations of potion mixing, which I performed. They wanted to hear the myths of Songhay cosmology, which I recounted. My time that year was limited and so I left them with the promise of return—to honor the trust that my mentor had bestowed upon me.

To meet my obligations to Adamu Jenitongo and his family, I returned to Tillabéri in March 1990. The wake my mentor's death produced a strong current of family strife. Adamu Jenitongo's relatives wanted to profit from his knowledge and power, which meant they fought among themselves. Moussa, the older son and Adamu Jenitongo's successor, warned me that jealous rivals in Tillabéri had promised to harm me. He immediately prepared a small pot of magic cake. We ate the contents to protect ourselves from the likelihood of sorcerous attacks. In the "black of night" I taught his sons what I knew about Songhay myth and medicinal plants. I quickly discovered that Adamu Jenitongo had lightened my burden. Before his death he had revealed a great deal to his sons.

After a few days in Tillabéri I returned to Niamey, vowing to return in a week's time. When I got to Niamey, conditions deteriorated. A car accident gave me a bruise above my right eye. When I attended a wedding celebration I felt the onset of malaria—weak legs, spinning head, delirious fever. My host suggested I stay in bed. He summoned his sister-in-law, a physician, who gave me a sulfa-based antimalarial drug, which made me break out in hives. I couldn't sleep. I dreamed that rivals would orchestrate for me a slow, tortuous death. The next morning I somehow managed to drag myself out of bed, hail a taxi, and visit the research center, where my colleagues suggested in no uncertain terms that I immediately return home. I then visited Soumana Yacouba, a Niamey healer friend who lived in a straw hut on the outskirts of Niamey, which, by then, had become a sprawling and populous town. Like my academic colleagues, he strongly suggested that I return home.

"Your path has been spoiled," he said. "You didn't pay attention this year. There are people who wish you ill, but you didn't come to see me before you started your work. Your baba [Adamu Jenitongo] can no longer protect you from others. Next time, you'll come to my house before you begin your work. Go home and strengthen yourself."[6]

I didn't know what horrible things had taken hold of me. Some of my symptoms suggested a drug-resistant strain of malaria. All of my Songhay friends and colleagues, who knew the history of my apprenticeship in Niger, said that my path has been spoiled. Having learned of the pains that had streaked up my leg in the "black of night," they said that I had been shot with a magic arrow, a central weapon in *sambeli*, or attack sorcery. Those "arrows" are used to frighten, sicken, or kill the victim.

Weak, feverish, and frightened I decided to leave Niger at once. Before leaving two feverish days later, I again visited Soumana Yacouba, who gave me herbs and resins to combat what he called "a sickness that isn't a sickness." Medicines in hand, I took the midnight flight to Paris, spent one night there, and then returned to Washington, DC.

At home, I made herbal teas and burned resins to treat the "sickness that wasn't a sickness." Even so, fatigue and psychological depletion made it difficult to walk, let alone go about my professional business. I remained housebound for a long period of time. Finally, I mustered the courage to see a specialist in tropical medicine. I described my symptoms.

"Sounds like drug-resistant malaria," he stated. "We'll need a blood test to be sure."

His nurse drew some blood.

"I'll phone you in a few days with the results," the doctor said.

I returned home. Every day I drank herbal teas and burned resins. Several days later, the tropical medicine specialist phoned with the results of the blood work.

"The test results are inconclusive. You probably had a severe case of malaria. That's why you're so weak."

"So it was malaria?" I asked, hoping for a simple scientific result that would put my mind at east.

"We can't be sure. It probably was malaria." He cleared his throat. "It could have been something else."

I left Niger in March 1990. It took me eighteen years to gather the resolve to return.

6 ::: NEW YORK CITY, IMMIGRATION, AND THE WAREHOUSE

As I slowly recovered from "the sickness that wasn't a sickness" I thought a great deal about my mentor, Jean Rouch. Following our first meeting in August 1976, we remained in regular contact. He always had encouraging words for my research on Songhay religion and tried to convince me to study film with him in Paris. I would stubbornly tell him that my path was writing, and that I had no "eye" for film. Despite my stubborn streak, he asked me to visit him in Paris and, when possible, in Niger. Through our association I developed a critical eye for documentary film and learned a great deal about doing ethnographic fieldwork. In Niger he introduced me to his friends and co-conspirators, Damoure Zika and Lam Ibrahim. In Paris he invited me to screenings of some of his least-known films, asked me into his editing suite, presented me to his Paris associates, and introduced me to one of his mentors, Germaine Dieterlen.

Thinking about the rich experience of being a small part of chez Rouch in Paris and Niger, I decided to write a book about him. Most of the critical assessments of Rouch's oeuvre had focused on his work in documentary ethnographic film. In so doing critics had overlooked the depth and quality of Rouch's written ethnographic work, which, in my view, had been extraordinary. My rationale for writing The Cinematic Griot was not simply to publish a work about Jean Rouch's ethnographic work. Because my path, as the Songhay would say, had been blocked, I was too frightened to return to Niger to resume my work on Songhay sorcery. Having come to the end of one path, I moved forward in a different direction and spent two years reading and writing about Rouch's work.[1]

Toward the end of that project, I received a phone call from Dr. Wendy Wilson Fall, a fellow anthropologist and a veteran fieldworker in Niger, Nigeria, and Senegal. Wendy told me that Nigeriens had come to New York City and could be found on 125th Street, a major thoroughfare in Harlem.

So in the spring of 1992 I traveled to Harlem for the first time. Not knowing what to expect, I was nervous. On a Saturday afternoon, I stepped off the bus at the corner of 125th Street and Lenox Avenue and entered a veritable African market—in America! The din of melodic African languages from the Sahel, the Savannah, and the equatorial forest hummed in the urban air. Clouds of aromatic incense rose above the incessant traffic on 125th Street. People selling, buying, negotiating, and hawking goods streamed along the sidewalks, sometimes spilling over into the street. Amid this sensuous kaleidoscope of activity, I noticed a man selling trade beads from a card table he had set up on the corner.

"Are there men from Niger here?" I asked in French.

He pointed down the street. "Over there."

After walking a few paces in that direction, a man stopped me. "Who are you looking for?" he asked me in Songhay.

I responded in kind, which, for some bizarre reason, didn't seem strange to him. He then took me to meet Boube Mounkaila, a Songhay man from the Niger River village of Karma. Boube called himself a "specialist of bags." As it turned out, I knew several of his aunts and uncles in Karma and Tillabéri, where I had "sat" with Adamu Jenitongo. Boube called over several compatriots and ordered lunch, which a woman brought twenty minutes later—several Styrofoam containers filled with rice and a rich meat sauce—Senegalese *mafe*. We ate in silence. After drinking lots of water, we began an informal discussion that has continued—with periodic hiatuses—for more than twenty years.

In the early phase of the New York work, I sat with my merchant friends in the frenetic craziness of the outdoor African market on 125th Street. During its heyday in the early 1990s there might be one thousand African vendors selling goods on any given weekend. Citing "health" concerns and the complaints of tax-paying Harlem shop owners, Mayor Giuliani shut down the 125th Street market in October 1994. Many vendors elected to set up shop on a blacktop owned by the Masjid Malcolm Shabazz, the mosque founded by Malcolm X during the early 1960s. The first iteration of the Malcolm Shabazz Harlem Market emerged amid the political machinations of Rudy Guiliani's New York. In this way an informal and "illegal" market became regulated and "legal"—a revenue-generating New York City arena of commerce.

Like my African friends, I too moved operations from 125th Street, where I had been the Anasaara Alfaggeh (the White Cleric who filled out employment or immigration forms), to the Malcolm Shabazz Harlem Market. There I enjoyed many informal conversations about economics and politics in Niger and America as well as a unending series of delightful debates on American popular culture—Jerry Springer, rap music, and break dancing, to name a few. As the years slipped by I got to know a good number of traders, including successful international traders like El Hajj Tondi, a trading "father," who provided funds for dozens of trading "sons." He would "arrange" for their visas and give them an initial investment to pay for their travel and inventory. During one of my visits to Harlem he proposed that I take the State Department exam so he might have an "inside man" at a West African embassy, someone who might "fix" things for his "children."

On a visit in 1997 to the Malcolm Shabazz Harlem Market, I met El Hajj Abdou Harouna, who that day was visiting Boube Mounkaila.

When El Hajj Abdou said he came from Belayara, I wondered

if he were a Sugi, a subethnic group of that region. "They say that the Sugi," I said, "is the cross-cousin of the sohanci (sorcerer)."

"I'm a Sugi," he admitted, smiling at me.

"That means I should begin insulting you," I stated, a smile creasing my face.

Laughter shook El Hajj Abdou's body. He slapped me playfully on the shoulder. "Okay, let's hear one."

"Your mother," I began, "is so . . ."

He slapped his knee. "Please," he pleaded. "No more . . . no more."

"Are you sure?"

He looked at me intently. "Why are you wasting your time here at this market? Come with me to the Warehouse. We have real merchandise there—wood [masks and statuettes] and mud [terra-cotta figurines]."

"So I've heard," I said. "But my work is here."

"Come and see a real market," he insisted.

I resisted, but weakly because I wanted to see the Warehouse.

"I'm going to the Warehouse right now. Let's go."

We took the subway to Penn Station and then walked another mile or so to the Warehouse. El Hajj Abdou introduced me to his colleagues. On each subsequent visit, the art traders there welcomed me warmly. They invited me to sit, drink coffee, and talk. On one such visit in February 1998, El Hajj Abdou introduced me to his brother, Yaya.[2]

THREE

AWAKENINGS

7 ::: THE SHADOW OF SICKNESS

Like most people in the world, the Songhay-speaking peoples of Mali and Niger think a great deal about illness. How could it be otherwise for a group of people for whom chronic hunger and compromised living conditions shorten the life span? During my time in Niger, I never got used to the wails of young mothers who had lost a child to malaria, to a gastrointestinal infection, or to the yearly epidemic of meningitis. Premature death is no stranger to rural or urban Songhay people.

During one rainy-season visit to Adamu Jenitongo's compound in Tillabéri, torrential downpours filled a deep garbage pit with muddy water. While playing, Djamilla, Adamu Jenitongo's granddaughter, aged five, fell into the pit and drowned. The family mourned the little girl but soon resumed the struggle of daily life. When I expressed my sadness, Moru, Djamilla's father and Adamu Jenitongo's younger son, shrugged.

"It was her fate," he said without emotion. "It was her time."

As soon as I arrived in Tillabéri the next summer, Moru brought his son, Yacouba, aged three, to see me. Yacouba's eyes burned with fever. A deep cough rattled his tiny rib cage. His lack of appetite worried Moru.

"He's very sick," he confided to me, "but I don't have the money to buy medicine."

I gave him the equivalent of ten dollars to buy antibiotics. In Tillabéri, if you had the funds you could buy medicine at the local pharmacy. If you lacked money, your child might or might not survive. Moru bought the medicine and the next day his three-year-old son was on the mend.

"If you hadn't been here," he said, "my son could have died."

"You would have found a way to get the medicine," I suggested.

Moru said nothing more and we never again discussed the subject of illness or death.

The senselessness of easily prevented death in rural Niger challenged my American sensibilities. In my youth I had little experience with serious illness or tragic death. My grandmothers, Leah and Rose, both died in their sixties, one of a stroke, the other of a heart attack. Both of them had led relatively full lives. Neither of them suffered a slow painful death. My mother, father, and their siblings all seemed—at least to me—to be full of vim and vigor. The same might be said of my cousins. At family gatherings talk rarely drifted into discussions of illness or death.

The existential challenges of Niger, though, gave me much pause. I saw lepers begging for food, polio victims hobbling about the dusty streets. I met children confined to makeshift wheelchairs because a poorly trained nurse had given them an injection in the thigh that had damaged the sciatic nerve. Elephantiasis had swollen one friend's foot into a shapeless club. Remarkably and impressively, none of these people ever complained about their wretched state. None of them seemed depressed.

My confrontation with illness, misfortune, and tragic death in Niger, however, did not change my long-standing orientation to sickness and misfortune. I was not a Songhay person and would never become one. No matter the depth of suffering I witnessed there, I buffered myself in the village of the healthy.

Most of us live in the village of the healthy, which means that we take good health as a normal state of being. If we get sick, it is usually a temporary nuisance. We may take a course of antibiotics or rest for a week to get over an upper respiratory infection, but soon enough we return to our normal everyday routines and think nothing more of illness. Illness is certainly not central to most of our thoughts.[1]

Two bouts of serious illness thrust me for the first time into the village of the sick, a place where illness and death become your constant companion, a reality very close to the everyday experience of Songhay people. In 1990, as recounted in chapter 5, the sudden onset of a serious illness (high fever, weakness in the extremities, and a seemingly never-ending series of hallucinatory dreams that made sleep impossible) forced my evacuation from Niger. Physicians never discovered the source of the disorder that kept me housebound for almost two months.

My healer friends from Niger had other ideas. They said that jealous practitioners, believing I had learned too much about Songhay sorcery, had sent "sickness" to me. They said that a magic arrow had pierced my body. "You must go home," they said. "You must stay in bed." They gave me aromatic resins and herbs. "Burn the resins to purify your house," they said. "Mix the medicine in coffee, milk, or tea and take it until your strength returns." Fearing for my life, I had left Niger in March 1990.[2]

After my return to the United States and a slow recovery, an already recounted series of serendipitous events soon dropped me into the vibrant social life of Harlem, the scene of a wonderfully chaotic African street market on New York's 125th Street. As I worked on the manuscript that would become *Money Has No Smell*, my book about Africans in New York City, a routine physical in 2001 revealed an abdominal mass, the size of a grapefruit, a finding that ultimately led to a diagnosis of non-Hodgkin lymphoma (NHL), a hematological cancer. Once again, I feared for my life. I steeled myself for a regimen of chemotherapy, hair loss, nausea, CT scans, uncertainty, and an unanticipated sense of isolation.

In a very short period of time cancer disrupted my comfortable world of family and work. My oncologist gave me some understatedly frightening pamphlets that described a set of unsavory chemotherapy options.

"Read those," he said, "and come back in three weeks."

My choices left little room for optimism. Because I hadn't presented NHL symptoms, I could watch and wait for those symptoms to develop. I could also undergo standard chemotherapy, during which carefully regulated poisons would be dripped into my body. The final option was a new drug, Rituximab, a genetically devised substance administered after a standard chemotherapy session. In most cases Rituximab bypassed the healthy cells that chemotherapy drugs annihilated, reserving its toxicity for malignant lymphoma cells. I chose the last option. I wanted to confront NHL head on with the latest and most potent barrage of medicines.

Such life-changing decision making gave me stomach pains and produced nausea. As I approached my first chemotherapy session, I wondered about hair loss, mouth sores, bone pain, numbness in the extremities, and debilitating fatigue. If I managed to emerge from a long course of chemotherapy, how long might it be before I'd need more treatment? How long could I expect to live?

These questions haunted me throughout the chemotherapy experience. Considering the life or death scenarios that are associated with cancer and chemotherapy, you might think that cancer treatment experience is filled with serious dread. In my experience, it wasn't. Although I can't say that chemo pleased me physically, I found it psychologically stabilizing. Routine treatment had replaced the uncertainty of diagnosis. Sharing space with other cancer patients in the treatment room made me feel less alone. As chemotherapy drugs dripped into our bodies, a few patients dozed off in their reclining chairs. Some patients chatted with family members. Others read books or magazines. A few patients liked to joke with the oncology nurses.

I'll never forget one fellow patient, an exceedingly upbeat man whose malignant larynx had been removed. He wasn't speechless, though. He used an electronic device to communicate.

When he spoke, his voice quavered like a robot. This condition didn't prevent him from teasing the nurses and having a spirited conversation with me. When he left I asked one of the nurses about him.

"He's always in a good mood. We love him here—always smiling and joking and loving his life."

After the first few chemotherapy sessions, which in my case would last up to five hours, I would enter the treatment room looking forward to seeing the nurses and fellow patients. Even so, I wondered, as do all cancer patients who submit to the infelicities of chemotherapy, if I were going to get better. After six chemo sessions, my oncologist ordered a CT scan to look in on my abdominal tumor. The results were encouraging: a one-third reduction in the abdominal mass.

Maybe I'd somehow find my way along the sinuous path of cancer?

Soon after that CT scan, my Nigerien friends in New York, who had heard about my illness, phoned and insisted that I travel to New York City to visit them.

"But I'm going through cancer treatment," I complained.

"It doesn't matter. The trip will be good for you," they insisted.

And so Rachel, my partner, and I slowly made our way to the local AMTRAK station and took the train to Penn Station. Once in New York, we walked to the subway and took a train to Harlem, getting off on 116th Street. Slowly, we advanced to the Malcolm Shabazz Harlem Market. As soon as my friends saw my gaunt body, they swarmed around me. Some of them enthusiastically pumped my hand; others gave me bear hugs.

"Paul, God be praised."

"Paul, you look pretty good."

"Paul, I know that you will be okay. I know it."

Then Issifi, who comes from a family of Muslim clerics, asked all the Nigeriens—seven of them—to make a tight circle around me.

FIGURE 14.
An entrance
to the Malcolm
Shabazz Harlem
Market. Photo
by the author.

"Paul, we are going to do the *Alfatia* [prayer for protection], for you."

My friends extended their arms in front of their bodies, opening their palms toward the sky. They began chanting the prayer. At the end of the incantation, they slowly moved their open-palmed hands toward their faces, eventually putting their hands over their eyes to complete the ritual.

"Paul, you'll be fine," Boube Mounkaila said.

"I'll phone my father," Issifi said. "He'll say the Alfatia for you. He's a powerful man, Paul. You'll get well."

At that moment I felt deep love for my Nigerien friends whose humanity seemed boundless. That expression of love gave me hope for the future. I had the support of a loving family and a terrific group of friends and colleagues, but in the end I was like every cancer patient who ultimately faces her or his disease alone. Despite my feelings of isolation in the village of the sick, I was convinced in a fundamental way by the ceremony that I wasn't completely alone in the world. That sentiment gave me the courage to move forward on cancer's path.

In the ensuing months I withstood a series of five-hour

chemotherapy and immunotherapy sessions; a series of CT scans, which, given what you have to ingest, are never pleasant; and one PET scan for which you are injected with a radioactive dye. If that wasn't enough, the cumulative side effects of chemotherapy took their toll on my body—increased fatigue and bone pain. After nine months of treatment sessions the results of the PET scan suggested that my cancer was in remission.

"Congratulations," my oncologist said, slapping me on the shoulder.

"This calls for some champagne."

"Have a wonderful celebration. But before you go, I should mention maintenance therapy."

"I know. I know," I said, wanting to leave the cancer center. I had researched the benefits of getting additional Rituximab dripped into my body. Early research results strongly suggested that two years of additional Rituximab, which had mild side effects, could lengthen considerably the duration of remission. Maintenance therapy was no guarantee of ending the disease, for the experts mostly agreed that there was no cure for follicular lymphoma, the subtype of NHL that had produced my abdominal tumor. Given those odds, I knew that I would elect to continue treatment, once a week for four weeks, every six months.

Following my oncologist's pronouncement, I entered the nether world of remission, which is very much a space between health and illness. You feel fine, but know that your condition has no known cure. You have a disease, they say, that can be managed, but not overcome. I was neither terribly sick nor completely healthy.

When I told friends, family, and colleagues that I was in remission, they, like my oncologist, congratulated me.

"You beat it," some people told me.

"You stood up to cancer," others said to me.

"You're done with it, aren't you?" one person asked.

"You're a warrior," a few people suggested.

"You're now a survivor."

I didn't feel like a warrior who had survived a battle and I resented the label of "survivor," which extends the cancer as war metaphor in which patients are encouraged to kill their disease as if it were an enemy. How do you tell someone who is in remission, which means you have to think every day about the incurable nature of your disease, that you should be proud for having emerged victorious from a battle?

Very few people understood how I felt. I felt a silent bond, though, with other cancer patients. They knew the emotional horror of a cancer diagnosis, the strange fraternity of treatment, and the intractable uncertainty of remission. They knew what I knew. Even though we may have come from different economic, social, and ethnic backgrounds, cancer had dissipated our differences, leaving only a silent bond of shared knowledge and understanding.[3]

Long after my treatment ended, my West African friends in New York City continued to check in on my state of being, a series of interchanges that provided me profound emotional support. Their orientation to illness was more akin to my post-cancer thinking. They told me that illness is an integral part of life. It can never be conquered or defeated. They said that we live on borrowed time and because we never know when our time is up, we should live fully in the moment. If illness compromises our time in the world, they'd like to say, then accept those limitations and live as well as you can in your circumstances. Such counsel gave me the will to move on with my life in remission.

∷

"Illness," my mentor, Adamu Jenitongo, once told me, "is a great teacher." Until I faced my own mortality, I didn't have the experiential wherewithal to understand fully what he meant. My confrontation with cancer profoundly changed my orientation to life as well as to the practice of anthropology. I continued to conduct fieldwork among my West African friends in New York City, but my approach to ethnography had changed. Before my cancer experience, I saw life as a straight highway. I had professional goals and I thought that if I followed a straight unobstructed path from here to there I would accomplish a great deal—receive research grants, win awards, publish books, and move up the ladder of academic recognition. My ongoing experience with cancer, however, made me less concerned with the hustle and bustle of the here and now of the straight highway. Cancer compelled me to think more about a future that would evolve along the sinuous side roads of uncharted experience.

Having sat in a recliner as an array of toxic anticancer drugs dripped into my body, I sometimes wondered about the meaning of my life in the academy. What was the impact, if any, of the books I had written? Would my words bring comfort, insight, or amusement to those who might one day read them? Why was I doing anthropology? As I neared the end of the maintenance therapy regimen, I realized that in the future it would be important for me (a) to produce works (memoirs, ethnographies, and novels) accessible to multiple audiences of readers—texts that, in their openness to the world, might in some small way bring a little sweetness to someone's life; and (b) to mentor as many students and junior colleagues as I could—as a way of meeting the greatest obligation of the (Songhay) specialist: to pass on what she or he has learned to the next generation.[4]

I have lived in the stark shadows of sickness. At first, the shadows are fearful. But once you adjust to their presence, they can be revelatory. They've enabled me to see my own shadow as the immaterial aspect of my being. That awakened vision transformed the perception of my place in the world.

8 ::: THREE YEARS IN THE SHADOWS

When the economic climate brightened a bit in 2004, Yaya returned to New York City. In the space of five years, he had experienced two significant deaths in his family. As previously mentioned, his older brother, Abdou, had died in Niger in 1999, probably of cancer. His younger brother, Daouda, died in Abidjan, Côte d'Ivoire, in 2003.

When I saw Yaya at the Malcolm Shabazz Harlem Market, I asked about his younger brother.

"He got sick and died," he said.

His statement resembled the one he had made years earlier about his older brother.

"One day he was fine, and then he got sick. Two days later he died."

As he spoke discomfort lined Yaya's face. A lingering illness like that of El Hajj Abdou is fairly easy to explain. A person gets sick for whatever reason and gradually the illness overtakes her or his body, making him or her increasingly weak. In time the body tires of life, and the life force (hundi) eventually leaves the heart and slips into the air, bringing on death. Illnesses that provoke sudden death are more troublesome. In some cases Songhay say that these deaths can be attributed to fate. In other cases Songhay attribute sudden fatal illness to sorcery or witchcraft. How can you explain the sudden death of a young man in robust health?

"How terrible!" I said.

Yaya shrugged. Just as he didn't like talking about his wife and children, he refused to discuss the death of a loved one—

especially if his compatriots may have attributed it to sorcery or witchcraft. Although Yaya was a devout Muslim who had made the pilgrimage to Mecca, he, like many Songhay people, maintained traditional beliefs about witchcraft and sorcery.[1] During this period of time Yaya abandoned his trade in Bura terracotta figures, preferring to collect and sell antique Tuareg silver jewelry—much easier to transport and store. By trading jewelry Yaya could also avoid setting up shop at the Warehouse. Following the death of Ousmane Zongo, as previously mentioned, business activity there had understandably declined.

"There's nothing going on there," he admitted to me during our conversation. "I don't like it there."

"Does it remind you of your brothers?"

"Paul, you know that we don't talk of the dead. We avoid using their names."

"Sorry, Yaya." I should have been more careful.

Yaya stood up, signaling an end to our conversation—on a rather sour note.

"How much longer are you in New York?"

"Business is not good. I'll soon be headed for Niger and Côte d'Ivoire."

Indeed, between 2004 and 2007 Yaya spent most of his time in Niger or Côte d'Ivoire. My friends at the Malcolm Shabazz Harlem Market apprised me of his West African activities. They told me that Yaya's local businesses—an assortment of dry goods shops and a few transport vehicles—had performed well, but that El Haji missed New York. They also said that Yaya liked being at home with his family in Niger. During this long hiatus he occasionally came to New York but didn't allot much time for visits, which meant that for a period of years we didn't have the opportunity to meet or have phone conversations.

During the summer of 2007, however, Yaya spent most, if not all, of his time in New York City. Every time I wandered into the Malcolm Shabazz Harlem Market I found him sitting on a flimsy card-table chair in front of Boube Mounkaila's handbag shop. In typical Songhay fashion, I would ask after his health and the health of his family. In typical Songhay fashion he would reply.

"Tali fo si." (Not one problem.)

To which I would respond, "praise to God."

He did look a bit tired. The downward trend in the trading cycle had been difficult for Yaya. Having known him for almost ten years, I felt that I could talk to him a bit about his health.

"I'm just a little tired," he'd admit. "I didn't get much sleep last night." Then he would change the conversation to my health. "You look fit," he'd say. "How is your work?"

I would then discuss my teaching and he would talk about the decline of the market for African art.

Several months later during the fall of 2007, I returned to the Malcolm Shabazz Harlem Market to visit my friends. As always, they greeted me with affection and asked after my health and the health of my family. As usual I sat down in front of Boube Mounkaila's bag shop. Boube was working hard, stuffing newspaper into his bags so that they would maintain their shape. We talked as he worked.

I couldn't resist the apt Songhay proverb: "Even at rest the donkey has a burden on its back."

"True Paul, there is always work to be done, no?"

"How is the market?" I asked.

"The market is okay," he said, "but not great. We're getting by."

"And your kids?"

"They're good. My daughter is so smart. She likes science and math. They put her in a special school. She speaks Japanese with her mother and is learning Arabic at the mosque. My son is doing the same. He also does well in school."

Other Songhay and Hausa traders from Niger walked over to greet me and then returned to their shops. When Boube and I were alone, I asked after Yaya.

"Last time I was here, Boube, El Hajj Yaya looked tired. Is he okay?"

"God be praised," Boube answered.

"Is he okay or just tired?"

Boube looked around to make sure that our conversation would not be overheard. Among Songhay people public discussion of personal matters is frowned upon. "He's got high blood pressure, which isn't so bad, but now he's got cancer, Paul."

"Iri koy me te baani" (May God grant health), I said.

"Amin."

"How long?"

"Since the spring," Boube answered. "He goes to Metropolitan Hospital every two weeks for treatment. We help with his business and bring him food. He sleeps a lot in his room. When he has the energy, he comes here to be with us. He says that we give him energy."[2] He took a depth breath. "How is your health, Paul?"

"I have scans twice a year. Just had one, and I'm clean—no cancer."

"Praise be to God." Boube waved down a young man on a bicycle. "We should order lunch. You want Senegalese rice and fish?"

"Sounds good."

"This young man will place the order and bring it back to us." Boube said.

Thirty minutes later, the young man brought two Styrofoam containers. The cook had filled the large one with thiéboudienne (fish, rice, carrots, cabbage, and rice all cooked in a spicy tomato sauce). In the smaller container we found mafe, which, as previously stated, is a rich meat sauce served over rice. Soon the aromas of delicious food attracted a group of traders who brought chairs and placed them in a circle around the food that had been atop a makeshift table, a plastic crate that had been turned upside down and covered with a tablecloth fashioned from a black

FIGURE 15.
Typical lunch
at the Malcolm
Shabazz Harlem
Market. Photo
by the author.

plastic bag. Before eating we acknowledged our thanks for the bounty of food and dipped our plastic spoons into the sauces.

As usual we ate in silence. While we ate El Hajj Yaya walked up to our group and sat down on an empty chair.

We asked him to join in.

He thanked us but said he wasn't hungry.

"At least have a taste?" I suggested, following Songhay custom.

He grabbed a spoon and tasted a small amount of rice and fish. Then he put his spoon down, a sign that he would eat no more.

We continued to eat in silence.

When we had satisfied our hunger, Boube gave a bottle of spring water to each one of us. We drank and began to talk about the state of the American economy, American and Nigerien politics, and the drama of reality television, which my friends watched as often as they could. At the borders of our conversation, the sounds of Congolese music filled the air with rhythmic melodies that contrasted with the ever-present background thump of hip-hop.

In short order the traders got up from the makeshift lunch table and returned to their shops. Some of them prepared for *alula*, the early afternoon prayer. El Hajj Yaya remained in his chair, and I sat down next to him.

I asked after his health and the health and well-being of his family in Niger.

"I am well and they are well," he said. "I thank God for our well-being."

We looked at each other but said nothing, Although our relationship had spanned almost ten years, it was as if that was the first time we truly saw each other. For me it was a look of mutual recognition and mutual resignation—cancer had now touched both of our lives. It was time to talk.

"Boube told me," I began.

"Yes," he said shaking his head. "It's true. I've got cancer."

"Iri koy ma dogonaandi," I said. "May God lighten your burden."

He hunched his shoulders and grimaced.

"You've got pain in your bones, don't you?" I asked.

"You know about it, my friend?"

"I'm afraid I do, El Hajj."

He nodded. "When I came to New York in the spring, I started to feel bloated all the time. There was a dull pain in my gut. I couldn't eat. Then I started to see blood when I went to the bathroom."

"And you hoped that it would go away?"

He gave me a wry smile. "Exactly. Except for the high blood pressure, I've never been sick. I thought it was something that would pass, but it didn't." .

"So you went to the doctor?"

"There are two doctors in Manhattan who know about Africans. The one I went to spoke French. He said he had worked in Africa and he had African art in his office. He told me to get some tests at Metropolitan Hospital over on Ninety-Seventh and First

Avenue. He said that Metropolitan was a good place for immigrants and a good place for cancer care."

"You went and had some tests?"

"I went there. They took lots of blood and gave me a scan. A week later I met with a doctor there who told me that I had a tumor on my intestine."

"Has it spread?"

"No, but they wanted to start chemo right away. I get it every two weeks. They put in what they called a port and pass the drugs through it. I went for a scan last week."

"What did it show?"

"The tumor got a little smaller. They say that I'll need chemo for a long time."

"It's hard and it's lonely," I said.

"You know how much I like being with my wives and children. I miss them. I feel all alone here, but they say I need to stay in New York." He sighed. "I guess I'll stay."

Silence filled the space between us.

"This is no life, Paul. My bones ache. I have sores in my mouth." He opened his mouth wide, revealing a soft palette covered with black spots. "I used to love food, but I can't taste it anymore. I always feel like I have to vomit. I've got no appetite."

"I know what you mean, my friend. But if you give it some time, it will get better."

"That's what they tell me at the hospital." He looked at Boube who had sat down with us. "I can't do my business. I don't even feel like being with my friends here. I don't know what I'd do without Boube. He's been good to me."

"There's no need for talk like that, El Hajj," Boube said.

Knowing all too well the feeling of isolation that cancer provokes but also the important need for human contact, I offered to help Yaya. "When I went through treatment, I looked up a lot of information. I'll do the same for you. If you don't like the hospital or your doctor, I can find another cancer program in New York."

"I'm okay for the moment, but I don't know how much longer I can do the chemo," Yaya stated.

"I'll find out what I can and give you the information."

As El Hajj Yaya nodded his assent, his cell phone rang and he launched into a long business conversation in Songhay, French, Hausa, and Bamana. Shortly thereafter he stood up to take his leave. "I'm tired. Going home," he announced. Following Songhay custom, I accompanied him to the subway at 116th and Martin Luther King Boulevard.

"You have my phone number," I said. "If you need anything, call me. I'll be phoning you from time to time."[3]

: : :

After our meeting, El Hajj never phoned me. His silence didn't surprise me. Songhay people usually don't like to speak of illness or personal pain — especially to people who are not members of their family. Even so, I wanted to do what I could. When I was able to reach him, which wasn't that often, he said that he was doing better, but that the chemo continued to make him weak. He hadn't regained his appetite. Learning of his serious illness, his wives wanted him to return at once to Niger, but his oncologist insisted that he remain in New York to receive more treatment. If he didn't get more treatment, the oncologist said, the cancer would advance rapidly, which is another way of saying that he would die. Meanwhile, Yaya had had yet another CT scan. While the intestinal tumor had shrunk a bit more, the scan still detected a bulky mass. Given this state of affairs, his oncologist prescribed a new array of toxic chemotherapy agents. Perhaps a new mix of ingredients would eliminate what appeared to be a somewhat resistant tumor.

Later in the fall I saw him once again in front of Boube Mounkaila's bag shop. He looked tired, but not especially ill. He did not appear to have lost weight and still had closely cropped hair. He seemed to be well.

He wasn't.

As he sat down, Boube gave him some tea to drink.

I asked after his health.

He said that his hypertension had complicated the cancer treatment. "You know how it is, Paul, black people suffer from high blood pressure more than others. I've got a monitor. This morning my reading was 180/89." El Hajj Yaya took medication for hypertension, but could not remember its name. "What does it matter," he said, "I don't think it's working."

As previously mentioned El Hajj Yaya received all his medical treatment at Metropolitan Hospital.[4] "I like it over there," he said. "The treatment is free, and there are interpreters—even in the doctor's offices. They've got two-way speakers. That way, I know what the doctor is saying and the doctor understands me. I've got a French interpreter, but there are also Wolof and Hausa interpreters. You know, I've been very well treated. That doesn't happen in hospitals in Niger."

"So what are your plans?"

"They say I'm getting better and that the treatment will be finished in another three months. Then they'll do some tests. But they think I'll need more treatment in the future."

"And Niger?" I ask.

"I'm missing Niger very much, but I'm not sure what I can do. They're worried about my high blood pressure. I don't know if I can go back to Niger any time soon. If I die, I'm no good to my family, but I'm worried about them and they are full of fear."

A month later, El Hajj Yaya seemed more upbeat. He felt stronger and had regained his appetite. But the fate of his family continued to worry him. "I need to do more to take care of my family. Niger is poor—not enough rain, too little food. Here I can make $5,000 a month and take care of the entire family.

What I'd like to do is live back in Niger and come back every three months—for business and for medical treatment."

To that end, El Hajj Yaya said that the head oncologist at Metropolitan Hospital wanted to write him a letter outlining his medical needs—the need for him to get a checkup every three months. And if the checkup indicated a relapse, he could then get the treatment he would need. "It's good for me and it's good for business."

"What about your high blood pressure?" I asked. "Shouldn't you see a heart doctor?"

"I can see one of them in Niger. Niger has good heart doctors and I can get blood pressure medicine there."

"That would be terrific, my friend."

"It would be good. I can feel the tumor leaving my body. Before, I couldn't eat, and now there is no problem."[5]

: : :

I returned to New York City in late January and again in early February 2008. Boube Mounkaila surprised me when he said that El Hajj Yaya hadn't returned to Niger.

"Why not?"

"His treatment isn't going well. He finished it and they took a scan and said that the cancer was growing again. He's got to begin a new treatment with different drugs."

I phoned El Hajj Yaya at his West Ninety-Seventh Street apartment. He sounded groggy and said that the lack of progress had frustrated him. "They keep telling me I need more checkups," he said, "and that I need more treatment. I don't know when it will end. When will I be able to go back to Niger?"

"What about the people at Metropolitan Hospital?"

"I'm well treated. But they can't give my any answers."

"But, do you want me . . ."

"That's all. Good bye."

When I told Boube about this conversation, he said that El

Hajj Yaya didn't want to talk with anybody. "He goes to treatments and checkups and is too sick or tired to come out to see us. He doesn't even want to talk. We're happy to see him here, but he doesn't come to Harlem very much."

"Do you visit him?"

"Sometimes, but he doesn't want visitors either. He likes to go alone to the hospital. When he has treatment I stop by his apartment to see if he's okay."

"I wonder if he's getting the best treatment?"

"Don't know."

"I'll gather some information and send it to him. I'll also find out more information on medical visas." [6]

"That would be good, Paul."

I gathered information on the various cancer programs at Memorial Sloan-Kettering, the NYU Cancer Institute, and the NYU Clinical Cancer Center, with specific data on colorectal cancer clinical trials. The information was straightforward, and because El Hajj Yaya had an astute sense of the world—including, of course, the world of medicine, I thought the assembled information would be useful. So I sent a package to his Ninety-Seventh Street apartment.

I waited a few weeks and then phoned him to see how he was doing.

At first he couldn't figure who was on the line with him. "Paul?"

"You know, the American from the market?"

"Oh, that Paul," he said. "Forgive me, I had chemo yesterday and my head is spinning."

"How are you?"

"A little weak today."

"Did you get the information?"

"Oh yes," he said a bit more brightly. "God be praised. It's good you sent it."

"Let me know if I can help."

"I will," he said abruptly. "I've got to go." In my view, El Hajj Yaya didn't want his misery to infect the spirit of his friends and family—better to suffer in isolation and not burden others.

: : :

As the months flowed by El Hajj Yaya remained in New York City. Boube reported that El Hajj had found an attorney who tried to get him a US visitor visa for medical treatment. The lawyer worked on El Hajj Yaya's case but found that he didn't meet some of the stringent criteria you need to obtain a medical visa. Meanwhile, Yaya continued to receive regular cancer treatments at Metropolitan Hospital. Periodic CT scans suggested little progress in his "battle" against cancer. Boube thought that El Hajj Yaya was depressed. Why else would he spend so much of the time alone in his apartment?

From the summer of 2008 until the end of the year, I traveled infrequently to New York City. I phoned my friends to catch up with them and ask after their health and their families. I tried to reach El Hajj Yaya, but his phone seemed turned off—at least when I called him. I left messages to let him know that he was in my thoughts. Boube Mounkaila, who saw him from time to time, said that El Hajj was frustrated with the course of his treatment. When the results of the CT scans demonstrated little progress toward remission, the oncologists at Metropolitan Hospital tried yet another a new mix of drugs to see if they might have a better effect. Meanwhile, El Hajj Yaya's bone pain had increased and his fatigue had deepened.

As I mentioned in chapter 3, in February 2009 I traveled to the Republic of Niger to gather information on the lives of those Nigeriens who worked in New York City but had decided for any number of reasons to return to Niger. In their absence, what had become of their families? Was it difficult to resume a "routine" life in Niger if you had spent years in New York City? Accordingly I spent many hours in the Grand Marché of Niamey, Niger's capi-

FIGURE 16.
A young man's
offering in
the Grande
Marché of
Niamey, 2009.
Photo by the
author.

tal city, talking with many of Les New Yorkais, the appellation given to Nigeriens who had made a "heroic" return from New York.

During that sojourn I also traveled to the famous market of Belayara with a group of students from Boston University who were spending a semester abroad in Niger. The students wanted to experience a colorful and vibrant African market. I joined them to see the hometown of my friend, El Hajj Yaya Harouna.

On a torrid February day that signaled an early beginning to the unforgiving Nigerien hot season, we drove into Belayara. I accompanied the students on a stroll through the market, enjoying some banter in Songhay about market conditions, the quality of market food, and the state of the weather.

As the students continued their market stroll, I peeled away from the group and asked some people if they knew where El Hajj Yaya Harouna's house was located. No one seemed to know. On a side street, I found an old man. Years of exposure to sun and wind had faded the white of his robes. A diet of millet and milk had made him gaunt. The dust had dulled his black eyes. I asked him if he knew my friend.

"You mean the brothers who went to America?"

"Exactly."

"I'll take you to their compound, but I don't think anyone is there." He took me down a dirt path bordered by high mud-brick walls and stopped in front of a door fashioned from corrugated tin. It was padlocked.

"No one home?" I asked.

"Looks like they're all in Niamey," he said. "The only time they come here is during the rainy season when they plant millet."

"So is this the house of El Hajj Yaya and El Hajj Abdou?"

"I'm not so sure," the old man admitted.

Disappointed, I walked toward the livestock section of the market and phoned El Hajj Yaya in New York. On that day, he picked up.

"El Hajj Yaya?" I said. "Are you there?" I said in Songhay.

"Yes," he said in a weak voice.

"It's Paul. "I'm calling from Belayara, your hometown. It's market day."

"Great God! You've seen the market," he said in a stronger tone. "You're phoning me from the Belayara market?"

"It's a huge market and it's very lively. I'm so glad I came."

"I miss it and miss Niger," he lamented.

"I tried to find your compound, but couldn't," I admitted.

"That's okay, my friend. It's good to hear your voice and to know that you went to my hometown and phoned me from there. It means a lot."

"How are you?"

"It's the same for me, my friend. The same. I live day to day, hoping to get enough strength to come home to Niger. I want to see my family again."

"May God will it!"

"Amin," he said. "Thank you."

That was the last phone conversation I had with El Hajj Yaya for a very long time. I returned to New York in March of 2009 and saw him for a short time at the Malcolm Shabazz Harlem Market. He talked business with the other traders but did not want to discuss his health or his plans for the future. After that visit I didn't see him or talk with him for many months. When I talked with Boube, he told me that El Hajj Yaya's condition hadn't changed. To make matters more severe, his illness had provoked a steep decline in his trading business. He couldn't arrange shipments or meet with clients. In fact, he entrusted his jewelry to others, hoping they might make a profitable sale. Boube said that Yaya was too weak to return to Niger, where in the presence of family and friends, he might emerge, if only for a little while, from three years in the shadows of illness.

9 ::: A REMARKABLE CONVERGENCE

I n my years as an anthropologist I have long held the assumption, which is perhaps a tad naive, that anthropologists could transcend the cultural gulf of difference that separates them from their others. I assumed that if you learned to speak the other's language fluently, your linguistic competence would be a strong indication of deep cultural respect, which could, in time, foster profound understanding and friendship between peoples defined by difference. That assumption compelled me to deepen my knowledge of the Songhay language. I studied proverbs and learned to talk about little-discussed cultural matters—the names of plants, the use of spices in Songhay cooking, expressions associated with farming and healing. The use of these specialized elements of the Songhay language usually impressed my interlocutors. They praised my command of the Songhay language. In markets the anomaly of a white man speaking "old" Songhay attracted crowds of onlookers.

"Where did you learn Songhay?" a few people would ask.

"You speak Songhay better than me," some would say with not a small degree of exaggeration.

When I "did" the famous market of Ayorou on the banks of the Niger River not far from the border between Niger and Mali, crowds of young people would come to listen to me bargain for a beautiful handwoven Songhay blanket. One day a man from Mehanna, the Songhay town where I conducted my early fieldwork, joined the crowd of Ayorou onlookers.

"Who is this white man who speaks Songhay?" someone asked.

"He's our white man," the Mehanna man chimed in.

The long-term relationships I established in the field also reinforced the assumption. I studied with my teacher Adamu Jenitongo for more than seventeen years. During that time I felt that we had developed an intimate bond—the loving ties of a father to his son. We had, or so I thought, bridged the wide cultural gulf that had separated us.

In 1988 I mourned his death, which not only brought to an end the life of a wise man but also changed my life as a field anthropologist. After his death, how could I go on with my work in Niger? Who could replace my mentor? I tried to do new fieldwork there, but as recounted in chapter 5, the situation in Tillabéri quickly deteriorated.

Despite my disappointments in Niger, I carried the same assumption with me to New York City. Although I never developed a relationship there that resembled the deep bonds I had shared with Adamu Jenitongo, I still felt that my linguistic and cultural knowledge of things Songhay might enable me to establish friendships that bridged the gulf of social and cultural difference. I liked the fact that in New York City my Nigerien friends called me "brother" and said that I spoke Songhay like a native. I especially liked it when they bragged about me to their customers.

"He's lived in my village."

"He knows our history."

"He's a *boro hano*" (a pure/good person).

When my friends said, "He's really a Songhay," I would respond: "Even if a log has been in the river for one hundred years, it can never become a crocodile." I'd follow that proverb, which would invariably provoke much appreciative laughter, with affirmations that I was and would always be an American.

My friends would disagree, which would quietly reaffirm the premise that I was somehow different from other white people. One day in 2004 a phone conversation weakened the foundation of that assumption. I phoned Issifi Mayaki, who has been one of my long-standing Nigerien friends in New York. Issifi and I shared a passion for political discussion but also had enjoyed long and intense debates about religion and culture. We often talked about racism and the general American ignorance about Africa and Africans. He liked to call me his "brother."

After several rings, Issifi's real brother, whom I hadn't met, picked up the phone.

I introduced myself.

In the background I heard Issifi ask who was on the phone.

His brother said, "Paul."

"Oh, that's the white man," Issifi said, not knowing he had been overheard. Moments later, he picked up the phone and said: "Paul! How are you, my brother?"

For me that incident underscored powerfully that the relationship of nonnative anthropologists to their others is vexingly complex. In a short essay in 2005 I wrote about my immediate reaction to the incident, coming to the conclusion that

> my particular capacities as a fieldworker or as a human being could not alter an always already set of racially defined sociological boundaries—of pre-colonial and colonial culture—established and solidified years before I had set foot in Niger. . . . How disappointing it is for ethnographers to admit, and in my case it was a grudging admission, that the relationships that they develop in the field, while close, are, in fact, not usually as special as they might think.[1]

One phone conversation did not dispel the feeling that my experiences in the Songhay worlds of sorcery and trade nonetheless had put me in a different category, a category in which a set of common understandings gave me insights into the social realities of my friends. And yet the applicability of the oft-quoted proverb never seemed stronger: "Even if a log floats in the river for one hundred years, it can never become a crocodile."

This clear-sighted set of field expectations didn't alter the texture of social relations with my Nigerien friends in New York City. We liked one another and we shared much laughter and pleasantry. Our ties continued to be mostly instrumental. They wanted me to buy things from them or send them clients. Sometimes they asked me to write them letters or find them an honest immigration attorney or a first-rate French-speaking physician. As any anthropologist doing research, I, of course, wanted to hear their stories so I might try to try to represent their experiences in America. In that way I could not only enhance my academic profile but could also help to create the space for an edified conversation about African immigrants in America.

My grudging realizations neither diminished the richness of my ethnographic experiences nor altered the sensuous texture of my ethnographic stories. Although I thoroughly enjoyed my long-standing relationships with my Nigerien friends in New York, I believed there were distant existential boundaries we would never cross.

These insights had little bearing on my relationship with El Hajj Yaya. We would see each other periodically in New York, and I would phone him from time to time. When he got sick, I was surprised that the nature of our relationship hadn't changed, given my experience in the world of cancer in which fellow patients experienced a silent bond. Indeed, the realities of cancer, in fact, probably compelled him to isolate himself. I understood why he would want to do so. I strongly believe that no matter the extent of your network of social support—and in my case the network was substantial and strong—cancer patients ultimately confront their disease alone. No one can feel your physical or existential pain. Sometimes it is simply better to retreat into the solace of solitude. And yet such solitude creates its own version of emotional pain. You want the love and support of family, but such love and support can often be unbearable. Such are the conundrums of the cancer patient.

In October 2010 I once again visited my West African friends at the Malcolm Shabazz Harlem Market. Because he spent so much time alone in his apartment, I didn't expect to see Yaya that day. And yet there he was sitting on a metal chair in front of Boube Mounkaila's "leather" handbag shop.

He looked tired. He mentioned that the chemotherapy drugs had reduced the size of his tumor and that his physicians had been cautiously optimistic about his prognosis. After almost three years of on-again, off-again chemotherapy, they wanted El Hajj Yaya to continue treatment to "manage" the cancer. That day we spoke vigorously about politics in the United States and Niger as well as about the twists and turns of the global economy. As always, I found Yaya an admirable man. In the face of what seemed like terminal cancer, I admired his dignity and stoic persistence.

When the other traders in our discussion group moved away to tend to their shops, El Hajj Yaya beckoned me closer. He looked deeply into my eyes and touched my hand.

"Paul," he said solemnly, "I'm going home."

Given our recent history, this intimate statement provoked a surprise that quickly dissipated into a profound silence of mutual recognition. Like two cats perched on a wall, we sat motionlessly and let the statement sink in. He nodded his head and we sat for a few moments holding hands, a sign of deep friendship in West Africa. People strolled by. The din of conversations hung in the background. The sweet smell of Bint al Sudan perfume filled the air.

That moment was just a spark of time, a perfect instant of profound mutual comprehension and experiential convergence. For just that moment I knew what he knew and he knew what I knew. We had crossed a distant existential boundary and entered a new space of awareness. It was what Martin Buber had brilliantly called an I-Thou moment of deep dialogue.[2]

We savored the moment. We knew it would be the last time we would see each other. In that moment of resignation, I felt a profound sadness. I don't know if El Hajj Yaya felt the same sadness and resignation.

He stood up and walked toward the market exit. A few paces from me, he turned around. "I leave in two weeks," he said in an even tone. He walked away—back to a life lived with pride and dignity.

So Yaya returned to Niger. I departed for my home in Wilmington, Delaware. He went back to his family and local businesses. I soon found myself once again among family, friends, and colleagues.

Boube filled me in on what happened to El Hajj Yaya after his return to Niger. In the absence of chemotherapy treatments, cancer quickly took hold of his body. He found it difficult to eat. He found it increasingly painful to walk. A month after his arrival he took to his bed. Friends and relatives came to the family compound to pay their respects. They talked about wonderful things—travel, El Hajj Yaya's life in Abidjan and New York, his considerable success in the world of trade. In this way, people bestowed upon him the cultural honor that befits a traveler, a restless taker of risks.

He died on January 1, 2011.

: : :

At our last meeting Yaya and I experienced a rare point of existential convergence, a perfect storm of mutual comprehension. Like all peak experiences in life, this one lasted only a few moments; for me those moments are unforgettable. Those moments changed me. They reaffirmed in me the belief that human beings from different backgrounds can overcome substantial differences and establish deep bonds of mutual comprehension.

Those last instants with Yaya also enabled me to understand more fully what Adamu Jenitongo had taught me a long time go:

"illness is a great teacher." For a long period of time, I thought that his statement referred to how sorcerers move forward on their path. It is through illness—sometimes natural, sometimes brought on through sorcerous acts—that the apprentice moves forward on her or his path of power. If you respond to illness with respect and dignity, you are ready to learn about more powerful rites and more profound truths. If you are not up to the challenge that illness presents, your journey ends at the fork in the road where your teacher guides you to another path. After the last meeting with El Hajj Yaya, I knew that illness was not only a great teacher but also a great leveler. When I sat in treatment rooms with fellow cancer patients, I realized that illness could wash away social differences. If you are a cancer patient hooked up to an IV, it makes no difference if you are a professor or a sanitation worker. From the patient's perspective, cancer does not draw boundaries of social class. In the treatment room cancer obliterates class distinctions, for everyone there is in the same situation—experiencing an unsentimental face-to-face confrontation with mortality. What I hadn't realized, though, is that the experience of serious illness also makes it possible for two people, defined by social, cultural, linguistic, and historical difference, to transcend their deep disparities, if only for a few intense moments, to experience a profound existential convergence. That convergence may have brought some existential closure to both of our lives. It may have given Yaya a measure of comfort on his journey to a dignified death. It gave me a sharpened appreciation of the vicissitudes of life on a path toward an uncertain future.[3]

EPILOGUE

THE QUEST FOR WELL-BEING IN THE WORLD

I began this book with a discussion of restlessness and the existential itch that compels us to try something new or make a daring choice. My teacher, Adamu Jenitongo, gave first shape to those thoughts about restlessness and change and comfort and well-being. He also liked to talk about the elusiveness of comfort and the ephemeral nature of well-being.

Such talk would have comforted El Hajj Yaya. Restless in the difficult nowhere of chemotherapy and social isolation, El Hajj Yaya chose to return to Niger. Seeing a final chance to grasp a measure of well-being, he chose a dignified death. His family, friends, and colleagues came to his bedside to express their respect for him and give him at the end of his life a sense of completeness and comfort.

But the quest for well-being is certainly not limited to how we decide to spend our final days. All of us experience the existential itch at various points of our lives. When I was fifteen, I wanted to take a young woman to see a film — my first date. To give myself a sliver of privacy, I went into the damp basement of my home to make the call. As I approached the phone, my heart raced. If she said that she didn't know me or if she turned me down, my world would be shattered. If she agreed to go out with me, I'd be filled with happiness and well-being. I took the chance.

She said "yes."

As it turned out, we had a terrible time, and I never saw her again. Because I wanted to experience such bliss again, restlessness prompted me to try my luck with another person who might take me to that special place where I'd once again feel the elation of well-being!

Anthropologists are no exception to the existential itch of restlessness that leads to a sense, albeit fleeting, of well-being. At the 2012 meetings of the American Anthropological Association, Edward Bruner presented a powerful paper, "The Aging Anthropologist," in which he discussed the increasingly disturbing relationship between aging and well-being. Reflecting on what it meant to present a professional paper at the age of eighty-eight, which, Bruner conceded, is "old," he stated:

> This is my private rebellion against the cultural stereotype of an old person in American culture, which I reject, as I struggle to construct my own vision and my own role as an active and creative old person.
>
> Doing anthropology, even writing this paper today, enhances my feeling of being in the world, restores my sense of self-worth, distracts attention from the physical infirmities of old age, and keeps me feeling more alive.[1]

Bruner's moving commentary underscores the existential centrality of our ever-present and contextually configured quest for well-being. Bruner's confrontation with the physical and emotional consequences of aging in American culture demonstrates how the capacity to change, the ability to displace yourself through time and circumstance, can give you the wherewithal to live well in your skin.

: : :

It is incontestable that well-being gives shape to the human condition. Despite the centrality of well-being to the comprehension of things human, it is surprising that anthropologists rarely write directly about it. For more than thirty years, we have focused our scholarly attention on social organization, symbolic meaning, research methods, the philosophical contours of representation, and the political ramifications of structures of violence, human rights discourses, and ethnographic engagement. Such preoccupation has left us precious little time to scratch our existential itches. When we do so, it is usually in an indirect manner. From an institutional perspective, discussions of human well-being are usually too introspective, too emotional, and too philosophical.

In the book *Life within Limits: Well-Being in a World of Want*, one of only a few ethnographies that directly consider well-being, Michael Jackson wrote: "My approach to the study of human well-being reflects a long-held assumption that while philosophers have often asked the most searching questions regarding the human condition, ethnographic method offers one of the most edifying ways of actually exploring these questions."[2] For Jackson, the most important component of ethnography is its intersubjective nature.

> Just as human experience is never simply an unfolding from within but rather an outcome of a situation, of a relationship with others, so human understanding is never born of contemplating the world from afar; it is an emergent and perpetually renegotiated outcome of social interaction, dialogue, and engagement. And although something of one's own experience—of hope or despair, affinity or estrangement, well-being or illness—is always a point of departure, this experience continually undergoes a sea change in the course of one's encounters and conversations with others.[3]

Indeed, the intersubjective texture of living life is underscored in *Yaya's Story*. As exemplified in Yaya's life, the personal and the professional are never separate because we are always interacting with and learning from others. In so doing, we not only learn about other ways of being but also learn much about ourselves. In so doing, we understand that the restless quest for well-being is both ever present and always changing. Following the courageous example of El Hajj Yaya, we realize that the quest for well-being can enable us to know what it means to be comfortable in our skins.

PERSONAE

Abdou Harouna: a transnational trader in African art from Belayara, Niger, and Yaya Harouna's older brother, who died in Niger in 1999.

Adamu Jenitongo: a powerful sorcerer and principal spirit possession priest in Tillabéri, Niger, who died in 1988.

Ag Gugul Ibegart: the "art doctor" at the African art Warehouse in New York City until 2002.

Angu Sandi: a transnational trader from Niamey and Dogondoutche, Niger.

Boube Mounkaila: a Nigerian merchant at the Malcolm Shabazz Harlem Market.

Daouda Harouna: a transnational trader in African art from Belayara, Niger, and Yaya Harouna's younger brother, who died in Abidjan, Côte d'Ivoire, in 2003.

Djibo Mounmouni: a healer who lives in Mehanna, Niger.

Goldie Berman: married Sidney Stoller in 1943; mother of Paul Stoller and Mitchell Stoller, who died in Boca Raton, Florida, in 2007.

Groggy Gurwitz: a dance teacher extraordinaire in Silver Spring, Maryland, in 1959.

Idrissa Soumana: the "chauffeur" of African art in North America, who currently "resides" in Chicago.

Issifi Mayaki: a Nigerien merchant at the Malcolm Shabazz Harlem Market.

Jean Rouch: French filmmaker and anthropologist and long-time student of the Songhay people, who died in Niger in 2004.

Leah Berman: Paul Stoller's maternal grandmother, who died in Silver Spring, Maryland, in 1962.

Mack Stoller: Paul Stoller's grandfather, who died in Silver Spring, Maryland, in 1985.

Moru Adamu: Adamu Jenitongo's younger son, who lives in Tillabéri, Niger.

Mounmouni Kada: Djibo Mounmoni's father and a healer and Paul Stoller's first initiator, who died in Mehanna, Niger, in 1980.

Moussa Adamu: Adamu Jenitongo's older son who lives in Tillabéri, Niger.

Moussa Boureima: a Nigerien merchant at the Malcolm Shabazz Harlem Market who returned to Niger in 2008.

Ousmane Zongo: the second "art doctor" at the Warehouse, who was tragically gunned down by the NYPD in 2003.

Paul Stoller: anthropologist, longtime student of the Songhay, and cancer patient.

Raymond Stoller: Paul Stoller's uncle and a physician, the Stoller family's model of success, who died in Detroit in 2013.

Rose Swartz: Paul Stoller's paternal grandmother, who died in Washington, DC, in 1965.

Sidney Stoller: Paul Stoller's father, who died in Delray Beach, Florida, in 1998.

Yaya Harouna: a transnational art trader from Belayara, Niger, and cancer patient, who died in Niamey, Niger, in 2011.

NOTES

PROLOGUE

1. See Steiner (1994), *African Art in Transit*, for an enlightening work on the marketing of African art in the United States. See also Taylor, Barbash, and Steiner's film *In and Out of Africa* (1992). The majority of African art traders are Muslims who have no cultural association with the objects they sell. Most of them told me that a mask or a figurine is a commodity—wood, mud, or iron—that embodies no spiritual power, or, for that matter, no spiritual danger to them. I wonder, though, if these statements represent the "party line." Most of the traders come from societies that practice spirit possession and sorcery and have grown up in communities in which witchcraft accusations are not uncommon. For major works on primitivism in African art, see Price 1989, 2007. For works on the aesthetics of (African) "primitive" art, see Errington 1998; Blier 1994, 1996; and Vogel 1997.

CHAPTER 1

1. The anthropological literature on the ethnic and gender dynamics of West African markets is a vast one. See Bohannan 1962 and Clark 1994, 2010; Grégoire 1992; and MacGaffey 1991.

2. For detailed descriptions of West African Islamic notions on the social texture of trade and trading, see Amselle 1971; Curtin 1975.

3. For studies of Muslim conceptions of trade, see Ebin 1990; Babou 2007; Mennan 1986; Stoller 2002.

CHAPTER 2

1. Among Songhay and Hausa people a truly rich man or woman possesses not only a healthy bank account but also a healthy network of associates, some of whom are tied to him or her through kinship, some of whom are linked through mutual economic incentive. See Stoller 2002; Grégoire 1992.

2. Plattner 1996, 6–7.

3. Plattner (1996, 30), referring to Raymonde Moulin, *The French Art Market* (New Brunswick, NJ: Rutgers University Press, 1987).

4. Plattner 1996, 126.

5. See Errington 1998. See also Marcus and Myers 1995; Price 1989.

6. Errington 1998, 68. See also Clifford 1988; Torgovnick 1990; Steiner 1994; Marcus and Myers 1995; Price 1989, 2007.

7. See Plattner 1996; see also Clifford 1988.

8. See Napier 1992.

9. See Stoller 2002, 2003.

10. See Hopkins 1973.

11. See Curtin 1975; Meillassoux 1991.

12. See Mennan 1986.

13. Mennan 1986.

14. See Amselle 1971; Stoller 2002.

15. See Stoller 2002, 2008.

CHAPTER 3

1. Field interviews in New York City, January 8, 2001.

2. Barry 2005.

3. The description of networks in a text for general readers merely scratches the surface of the complex anthropological and sociological studies of networks, which is vast. Much of the work has focused upon two domains of network relations: (a) the social texture of relatedness, and (b) the mathematical dynamics of linkages. Readers who would like an in-depth exploration of social networks might want to start with early work in anthropology that considered primarily the social textures of personal networks as exemplified in the classic works of Barnes 1954; Mitchell 1974; and especially Kapferer 1973. As the analysis evolved scholars refined their gaze to think how urban-rural ties or transnational ties might have an impact on network relations (see Weisner 1978 on urban-rural ties in Kenya and MacGaffey and Bazenguissa-Ganga 2000 on transnational links between France and Congo). By contrast, the study of whole networks tends to be abstract; scholars construct simulation models and sampling schemes that they use to delimit what they call network clusters or hubs (see Johnson 1994; Borgatti, Everett, and Johnson 2013).

4. See Taylor 2002.

5. According to Angu Sandi, Honda and Toyota automobile parts are readily available in Niger. Parts from other auto manufacturers are much more difficult to obtain, which makes it more profitable to ship Hondas and Toyotas. Interview with Angu Sandi, Niamey, Niger, February 5, 2009.

6. Interview with El Hajj Yaya Harouna in New York City, October 4, 2000.

7. See ICOM 1997.

8. Interview with El Hajj Yaya Harouna in New York City, October 18, 2000. In this discussion, El Hajj Yaya never talked about if he might be fearful of the existential consequences of disrupting a sacred burial site.

CHAPTER 4

1. The American fiction of, among others, Saul Bellow, Philip Roth, and J. D. Salinger wonderfully captures mid-twentieth-century urban Jewish culture's will to succeed in business and/or in intellectual endeavors. Two factors gave rise to my fascination with continental philosophy. The cultural environment evoked by the likes of Bellow, Roth, Salinger, and other writers pushed me toward literature and the arts. The experimental mores of the 1960s reinforced my desire to do something new and unexpected. Why not study philosophy and live the writer's life in an exotic place like Paris? Although my parents thought me unrealistic, they did not stand in my way—for which I am forever grateful. It took them many years to understand and appreciate my adventures on anthropology's path.

2. The impact of that early study of French phenomenology, especially the work of Merleau-Ponty, has had a lasting influence on all of my subsequent work in anthropology.

3. This story was the basis for a fictional account in *Gallery Bundu* (Stoller 2005).

CHAPTER 5

1. More detailed accounts can be found in Stoller 2004, 2008. Some of the ethnography was transformed into fiction in Stoller 2005.

2. See Stoller and Olkes 1987.

3. This period of work is adapted from Stoller 1989a, 1989b, 1992, 1995, 1997, 2004, 2008; Stoller and Olkes 1987.

4. For a more detailed description, see Stoller and Olkes 1987.

5. See Stoller and Olkes 1987; Stoller 2008.

6. See Stoller 1997, 11.

CHAPTER 6

1. See Stoller 1992.

2. See Stoller 2002.

CHAPTER 7

1. See Stoller 2004.

2. Stoller 1997.

3. Stoller 2004, 2008, 2013.

4. See Stoller 1997, 2005, 2013.

CHAPTER 8

1. There is a vast literature on the multidimensionality of African systems of belief. While Islam may appear to be prominent in many parts of North,

West, and East Africa, there exists in all these regions a substrate of pre-Islamic beliefs and practices. Consider the spirit possession brotherhoods in Morocco and Tunisia (see Crapanzano 1981; Kapchan 2007). Consider spirit possession and magical practice in Mali and Niger (see Stoller 1989a, 1995; Masquelier 2001, 2009; Gibbal 1982, 1984, 1994). Consider finally the blend of evangelical Christianity with non-Christian traditions in West, Central, and Southern Africa (see Werbner 2011; Jules-Rosette 1975; Engleke 2007). Given this context, it comes as no surprise that El Hajj Yaya would hold spiritual beliefs that would, at first glance, seem contradictory. Did he attribute his cancer to his selling objects extracted from a burial ground? Given my immersion in the world of Songhay sorcery, I struggle with this very question. Did my cancer come from exposure to DDT, a pesticide commonly associated with NHL, or is attributable to the work of a sorcerous rival in Niger? I don't know if El Hajj Yaya came to terms with this issue. I continue to struggle with it.

2. Interview with Boube Mounkaila in New York City, September 19, 2007.

3. Interview with Boube Mounkaila in New York City, September 19, 2007.

4. From the website of Metropolitan Hospital Center: "Metropolitan Hospital Center provides residents of East Harlem and neighboring areas with the most comprehensive medical services available, all at little or no cost to our patients. Patients have access to:

- Over 90 primary care and specialty services
- State-of-the-art Intensive Care Unit
- Comprehensive surgery department
- Physical medicine and rehabilitation services
- Radiology department equipped with the latest technology
- Behavioral Health Pavilion

Our wide range of services along with our high caliber staff makes us the provider of choice for the health care needs of the community."

5. Interviews with El Hajj Yaya Harouna and Boube Mounkaila in New York City, September 19, 2007, and October 18, 2007.

6. From the US Department of State's website on visas, here are some of the conditions that El Hajj Yaya needed to meet to obtain a US medical visa: "Generally, a citizen of a foreign country who wishes to enter the United States must first obtain a visa, either a nonimmigrant visa for temporary stay, or an immigrant visa for permanent residence. The visa allows a foreign citizen to travel to the United States port of entry and request permission of the U.S. immigration inspector to enter the U.S." The "visitor" visa is a nonimmigrant visa for persons desiring to enter the United States temporarily

for business (B-1), for pleasure or medical treatment (B-2), or a combination of both (B-1/B-2) purposes.

Important Notice: Recent changes to U.S. law relate to the legal rights of employment-based nonimmigrants under Federal immigration, labor, and employment laws. As a personal or domestic employee seeking to come to the U.S. temporarily (on a B-1 Visitor Visa), before your interview, it is important that you review the Nonimmigrant Rights, Protections and Resources pamphlet on our webpage.

Applicants like El Hajj Yaya would have to prove that:

- The purpose of their trip is to enter the U.S. for business, pleasure, or medical treatment;
- That they plan to remain for a specific, limited period;
- Evidence of funds to cover expenses in the United States;
- Evidence of compelling social and economic ties abroad; and
- That they have a residence outside the U.S. as well as other binding ties that will insure their return abroad at the end of the visit.

Suffice it to say that El Hajj Yaya did not meet the stringent criteria for a US visiting visa.

CHAPTER 9
1. Stoller 2005, 197–98.
2. See Buber 2000.
3. See Langer 2009.

EPILOGUE
1. Bruner 2012.
2. Jackson 2011, xi.
3. Jackson 2011, xiii.

REFERENCES

Amselle, Jean-Loup. 1971. "Parenté et commerce chez les Kooroko." In *The Development of Indigenous Trade and Markets in West Africa*, edited by Claude Meillassoux, 253–66. London: Oxford University Press.

Babou, Cheikh Anta. 2007. *Fighting the Greater Jihad: Amadu Bamba and the Founding of the Muridiyya of Senegal, 1853–1913*. New African Histories. Athens: Ohio University Press.

Barnes, John A. 1954. "Class and Committees in the Norwegian Island Parish." *Human Relations* 7: 39–58.

Barry, Dan. 2005. "In an Hour, a Life Ended, One Upended." *New York Times*, February 26.

Blier, Susanne P. 1994. *The Anatomy of Architecture*. Chicago: University of Chicago Press.

———. 1996. *African Vodun: Art, Psychology, and Power*. Chicago: University of Chicago Press.

Bohannon, Paul, ed. 1962. *Markets in Africa*. Evanston, IL: Northwestern University Press.

Borgotti, Stephen P., Martin G. Everett, and Jeffrey C. Johnson. 2013. *Analyzing Social Networks*. Thousand Oaks, CA: Sage.

Bruner, Edward. 2012. "The Aging Anthropologist." Paper read at the 2012 Meeting of the American Anthropological Association, San Francisco, California, November 14–19.

Buber, Martin. 2000. *I and Thou*. Translated by Ronald Gregor Smith. New York: Scribner.

Clark, Gracia. 1994. *Onions Are My Husband: Survival and Accumulation by West African Market Women*. Chicago: University of Chicago Press.

———. 2010. *African Market Women: Seven Life Stories from Ghana*. Bloomington: Indiana University Press.

Clifford, James. 1988. *The Predicament of Culture*. Cambridge, MA: Harvard University Press.

Crapanzano, Vincent. 1981. *Tuhami: Portrait of a Moroccan*. Chicago: University of Chicago Press.

Curtin, Philip. 1975. *Economic Change in Precolonial Africa: Senegambia in the Era of the Slave Trade*. Madison: University of Wisconsin Press.

Ebin, Victoria. 1990. "Commercants et missionaries: Une confrerie musulmane senegalaise à New York." *Hommes et Migrations* 1132: 25–31.

Engelke, Matthew. 2007. *A Problem of Presence: Beyond Scripture in an African Church*. Berkeley: University of California Press.

Errington, Shelly. 1998. *The Death of Authentic Primitive Art and Other Tales of Progress*. Berkeley: University of California Press.

Gibbal, Jean-Marie. 1982. *Tambours d'eau*. Paris: Le Sycamore.

———. 1984. *Guérisseurs et magiciens du Sahel*. Paris: Presses Universitaires de France.

———. 1993. *Genii of the Niger River*. Translated by Beth G. Raps. Chicago: University of Chicago Press.

Gottlieb, Alma, ed. 2012. *The Restless Anthropologist: New Fieldsites, New Visions*. Chicago: University of Chicago Press.

Grégoire, Emmanuel. 1992. *The Alhazai of Maradi: Traditional Hausa Merchants in a Changing Sahelian City*. Boulder, CO: Lynne Reinner.

Hopkins, Anthony G. 1973. *An Economic History of West Africa*. London: Routledge.

Howes, David. 2005. *Sensual Relations: Engaging the Senses in Cultural and Social Theory*. Ann Arbor: University of Michigan Press.

International Council of Museums. 1997. *Red List Report*. New York: United Nations.

Jackson, Michael D. 2011. *Life within Limits: Well-Being in a World of Want*. Durham, NC: Duke University Press.

Johnson, Jeffrey C. 1994. "Anthropological Contributions to the Study of Social Networks: A Review." In *Advances in Social Network Analysis*, edited by Stanley Wasserman and Joseph Galaskiewicz, 113–52. Thousand Oaks, CA: Sage.

Jules-Rosette, Bennetta. 1975. *African Apostles: Ritual and Conversion in the Church of John Maranke*. Ithaca, NY: Cornell University Press.

Kapchan, Deborah. 2007. *Traveling Spirit Masters: Moroccan Gnawa Trance and Music in the Global Marketplace*. Middletown, CT: Wesleyan University Press.

Kapferer, Bruce. 1973. "Social Network and Conjugal Role in Urban Zambia: Toward a Reformation of the Bott Hypothesis." In *Network Analysis: Studies in Human Interaction*, edited by Jeremy Boissevain and John Clyde Mitchell, 83–110. The Hague: Mouton.

Langer, Ellen. 2009. *Counterclockwise: Mindful Health and the Power of Possibility*. New York: Ballantine Books.

MacGaffey, Janet. 1991. *The Real Economy of Zaire*. Philadelphia: University of Pennsylvania Press.

MacGaffey, Janet, and Rémy Bazenguissa-Ganga. 2000. *Congo-Paris: Transnational Traders on the Margins of the Law*. Bloomington: Indiana University Press.

Marcus, George E., and Fred Myers, eds. 1995. *The Traffic in Culture: Refiguring Art and Anthropology*. Berkeley: University of California Press.

Masquelier, Adeline. 2001. *Prayer Has Spoiled Everything: Possession, Power, and Identity in an Islamic Town of Niger*. Durham, NC: Duke University Press.

———. 2009. *Women and Islamic Revival in a West African Town*. Bloomington: Indiana University Press.

Meillassoux, Claude. 1991. *The Anthropology of Slavery*. Translated by Alide Dasnois. Chicago: University of Chicago Press.

Mennan, M. A. 1986. *Islamic Economics: Theory and Practice*. Boulder, CO: Westview Press.

Mitchell, J. Clyde. 1974. "Social Networks." *Annual Review of Anthropology* 3: 279–99.

Morris, Brian. 1987. *Anthropological Studies of Religion: An Introductory Text*. Cambridge: Cambridge University Press.

Napier, A. David. 1992. *Foreign Bodies: Performance, Art, and Symbolic Anthropology*. Berkeley: University of California Press.

New York City. 2012. Metropolitan Hospital Center: Our Services. http:// www.nyc.gov/html/hhc/mhc/html/services/services.html.

O'Brien, Tim. 1990. *The Things They Carried*. New York: Broadway Books.

Plattner, Stuart. 1996. *High Art Down Home*. Chicago: University of Chicago Press.

Price, Sally. 1989. *Primitive Art in Civilized Places*. Chicago: University of Chicago Press.

———. 2007. *Paris Primitive: Jacques Chirac's Museum on the Quai Branly*. Chicago: University of Chicago Press.

Rouch, Jean. 1956. "Migrations au Ghana." *Journal de la Société des Africanistes* 26 (1–2): 33–196.

Steiner, Christopher. 1994. *African Art in Transit: On the Creation of Authenticity in the African Art Market*. New York: Cambridge University Press.

Stoller, Paul. 1989a. *Fusion of the Worlds: An Ethnography of Possession among the Songhay of Niger*. Chicago: University of Chicago Press.

———. 1989b. *The Taste of Ethnographic Things: The Senses in Anthropology*. Philadelphia: University of Pennsylvania Press.

———. 1992. *The Cinematic Griot: The Ethnography of Jean Rouch*. Chicago: University of Chicago Press.

———. 1995. *Embodying Colonial Memories: Spirit Possession, Power, and the Hauka in West Africa*. New York: Routledge.

———. 1997. *Sensuous Scholarship*. Philadelphia: University of Pennsylvania Press.

———. 2002. *Money Has No Smell: The Africanization of New York City*. Chicago: University of Chicago Press.

———. 2003. "Circuits of Art / Paths of Wood: Exploring an Anthropological Path." *Anthropological Quarterly* 76 (2): 207–35.

———. 2004. *Stranger in the Village of the Sick: A Memoir of Cancer, Sorcery, and Healing*. Boston: Beacon Press.

———. 2005. *Gallery Bundu: A Story about an African Past*. Chicago: University of Chicago Press.

———. 2008. *The Power of the Between: An Anthropological Odyssey*. Chicago: University of Chicago Press.

———. 2013. "Cancer Rites and the Remission Society." *Harvard Divinity Bulletin* 41 (Winter/Spring): 69–75.

Stoller, Paul, and Cheryl Olkes. 1987. *In Sorcery's Shadow: A Memoir of Apprenticeship among the Songhay of Niger*. Chicago: University of Chicago Press.

Synnott, Anthony. 1993. *The Body Social: Symbolism, Self, and Society*. New York: Routledge.

Taylor, Lucien, Ilisa Barbash, and Christopher Steiner. 1992. *In and Out of Africa*. Berkeley: University of California Media Extension.

Taylor, Mark. 2002. *The Moment of Complexity: Emerging Network Culture*. Chicago: University of Chicago Press.

Torgovnick, Marianna. 1990. *Gone Primitive: Savage Intellects, Modern Lives*. Chicago: University of Chicago Press.

United States Government. 2012. "Temporary Visitors to the United States." http://travel.state.gov/visa/temp/temp_1305.html.

Vogel, Susan Mullin. 1997. *Baule: African Art, Western Eyes*. New Haven, CT: Yale University Press.

Weisner, Thomas. 1978. "The Structure of Sociality: Urban Migration and Rural Ties in Kenya." *Urban Anthropology* 5: 199–223.

Werbner, Richard. 2011. *Holy Hustlers, Schism, and Prophecy: Apostolic Reformation in Botswana*. Berkeley: University of California Press.

INDEX

Abdou Harouna, 2, 3, 19, 24, 34, 103–4, 129; and expansion of African art trade, 33
Abidjan, 19, 22, 77, 116
Adamu Jenitongo, 1, 80–83, 92–93, 107, 114, 136; apprenticeship with, 93–96; death of, 96
Adelberg, Michael, x
African masks, 4, 5
Ag Gugul Ibegart, 35; as African art doctor, 35–36
Alderman, Sarah, xi
Amselle, Jean-Loup, 31, 146
Angu Sandi, 39–48, 146
anthropology, 7, 8, 115; and fieldwork, 131–34
Armory Show, 27

Behar, Ruth, x
Babou, Cheikh Anta, 145
Bacigalupo, Anna Mariella, xi
Baule people, 22
Berman, Goldie, 63, 66
Blier, Susan Preston, 145
Bohannon, Paul, 145
Boube, Gado, 56
Boube Mounkaila, 59, 102, 111–12, 117–18, 148
Boulhassane, Boureima, 86–88
Brent, T. David, xi
Bruner, Edward, 140, 149
Buber, Martin, 141, 149
Bura reliquary, 53; looting of, 54–58

Chernoff, John, xi
Chomsky, A. Noam, 84
Christie's, 25
Clark, Gracia, 145
Clough, Paul, x
commerce, 7; and Yaya's path, 7–8
Cote d'Ivoire, 3, 19, 22, 29, 32, 116
Croix d'Agadez, 24, 25
CT scans, 109, 111, 123, 127

Daouda Harouna, 8, 22, 24
DeSousa, Valerian, x, xi
Djibo Mounmouni, 90; and the initiation of Paul Stoller, 90–92
Dumont, Jean-Paul, x

Errington, Shelly, 145

Fall, Wendy Wilson, 102
Fernandez, James W., x
France, 32, 45; Nigerien attitudes toward, 45
Fulan people, 17

Gendelman, Beverly, 63
Ghana, 32
Gottlieb, Alma, x
Graham, Philip, x
Grande Marché of Niamey, 43, 45
Guro people, 3, 22; masks of, 23
Gurwitz, "Groggy," 68, 69

Hagberg, Sten, x
Hannerz, Ulf, x